PERPLEXING PUZZLES

CRYPTIC CHALLENGES

EQUIVOCAL ENIGMAS

First published by Parragon in 2012

Parragon
Queen Street House
4 Queen Street
Bath BA1 1HE, UK
www.parragon.com

Produced by Tall Tree Books
Written by Rob Colson
Designed by Malcolm Parchment

Cover design by Michael Duffy

ISBN 978-1-4454-7583-7

Printed in Indonesia

Picture credits: (shutterstock unless stated)
2tr Steve Mann, 2tl donatas1205, 2–3 Atelier Sharaku, 4tl donatas1205, 4–5 chris scredon/istock, 5 Baloncici, 5 Zanico/dreamstime, 6–7 shalunts, 7b John Kershner, 7r shalunts, 8tl donatas1205, 8–9 Lebazele/istock, 9r Péter Gudella, 8–9 Eleonora Kolomiyets, 10 T.W., 10–11 Steve Mann, 11r Steve Mann, 12 Thorsten Schmitt, 12–13 stocknshares, 13br Steve Mann, 14bl Steve Mann, 14–15 Steve Mann, 15r Anna Jurkovska, 18b PILart, 18–19 titelio, 19r Steve Mann, 19c Mike Bentley/istock, 21l–r marekuliasz, 23t Yurchyks, 24 markrhiggins, 25r Sbelov, 26 donatas1205, 27r fuyu liu, 30–31 Tarek El Sombati/istock, 31b Sergio Schnitzler, 33c Stephen Morris, 32–33 Novitech, 34 granata1111, 34 William Bacon, 35tr fuyu liu, 34–35 fuyu liu, 35b Valentin Agapov, 38l markrhiggins, 38b dreamstime, 38–39 Chereshnya/dreamstime, 39 Tischenko Irina/dreamstime, 40 IDAL/dreamstime, 42 Stephen Coburn, 42–43 donatas1205, 43b jörg röse – oberreich, 44 tanewpix, 45 Feliks Kogan, 46 loriklaszlo, 46b colillusion bricks, 46–47 Fotana, 50 Selahattin Bayram/istock, 52tl Crom, 52 Steve Mann, 54–55 Marafona, 56tl Atelier Sharaku, 57br Eleonora Kolomiyets, 58b Helen Cingisiz, 60–61 Lebazele/istock, 61tr androfroll, 64 shutterstock, 65tl BW Folsom, 66bl Worldpics, 66b Orla, 69 Margo Harrison, 70cl SVLuma, 71tr Ron Peigl/istockphoto, 74–75c Arie v.d. Wolde, 74–75b Eleonora Kolomiyets, 75br Steve Mann, 76tl tanewpix, 76–77 Péter Gudella, 76bc Mike Bentley/istock, 77c Marilyn Volan, 78–79t stocknshares/istock, 79tr Stephen Coburn, 80tl holbox, 82r Kesamasek, 86–87 Lebazele, 88b Guy Shapira, 88–89 chris scredon/istock, 93bc Nicemonkey, 94bl Alexander Ishchenko, 95c khz, 96l–r RoxyFer, 98–99tc Steve Mann, 100b Evgeny Karandaev, 100l Gordon Galbraith, 100–101tc titelio, 101r Worldpics, 101b Jasenka, 104l Krasowit, 104c oriontrail, 105rc John Kershner, 105rb markrhiggins, 108–109 Brad Remy, 110 Ivan Bondarenko, 111 bioraven, 118 Michael Klenetsky, 122 Nejron Photo, 136 Baloncici, 140 Jim Barber, 142 nando viciano, 144 Transition, 146 Gordana Sermek, 158 Sergik, 161 Benjamin Haas, 163 Africa Studio

Remember These From School?

For some of the puzzles, you will need a few simple mathematical formulas on hand.

Pythagoras' theorem for right-angle triangles is the most important one:

The square of the hypotenuse is equal to the sum of the squares of the other two sides.

To figure out the area of a circle, you need the number π (pi), which equals about 3.14.

The area of a circle equals πr^2, where r is the radius. The circumference of a circle equals $2\pi r$.

At one point, you'll need to think about similar triangles—remember that if the internal angles of two triangles are the same, the proportions between the lengths of their sides will also be the same.

INTRODUCTION

Beware! Thinking about these 300 brainteasers may well make your head hurt. Like a devious magician, the puzzles will try to fool you by misdirection, using subtle cues to lead your thinking in completely the wrong direction. All may not be as it first appears.

The puzzles in this book will test your ability with numbers, logical reasoning, spatial awareness, and powers of imagination. There are paradoxes dating back to the ancient Greeks, classic conundrums from nineteenth-century puzzlers, such as Sam Loyd and Henry Dudeney, plus modern takes on old themes and brand new teasers. Keep a box of matches handy. Dotted through the book are some fiendish problems where you're going to need them.

Don't worry if you cannot see how to do all of them. Many of these puzzles are easier than they look, but there are also some really tough ones, which will test even the most experienced puzzler. All the answers are in the back, but try not to peek until you've thought long and hard about them. The pleasure of knowing the answer is made that much sweeter by having discovered it for yourself.

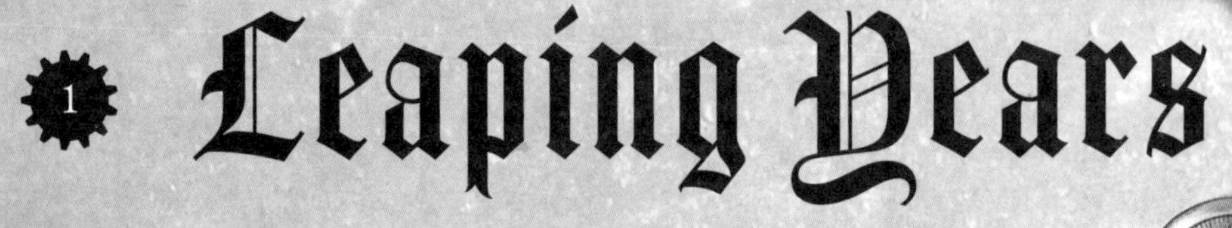

1 Leaping Years

Dr. and Mrs. Maxwell's son was born on Monday, February 29, 1892. How old was he the next time his birthday fell on a Monday?

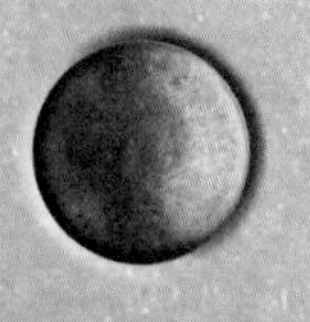

Solution on p. 175

2 Mailbox

Can you connect the dots to make the shape of an envelope without lifting the pen from the paper?

Solution on p. 175

3

SECRET MESSAGE

Connie needs to send a secret message in a box to Daniel on the other side of town. They both have a padlock, but for security reasons, they only have keys for their own padlocks. How can Connie send the message to Daniel in such a way that Daniel can open the box, but any nosy messenger cannot look inside?

Solution on p. 175

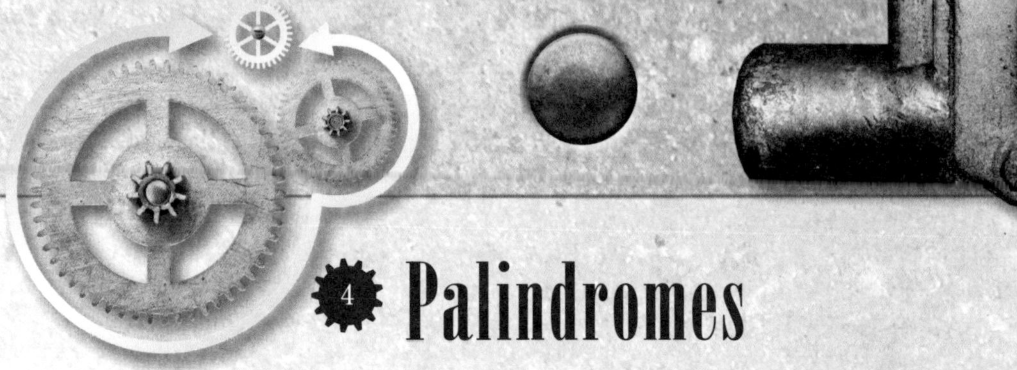

4 Palindromes

Phileas Fogg notices that he has traveled 15,951 miles since leaving London on his around-the-world journey. He sees that this number is a palindrome (reads the same from left to right as from right to left) and decides to keep an eye open for the next one. Two days later, he notices that his distance is again a palindrome. How far did he travel in those two days?

Solution on p. 175

5 TWO SQUARES

Move two matches to make two squares.

Solution on p. 175

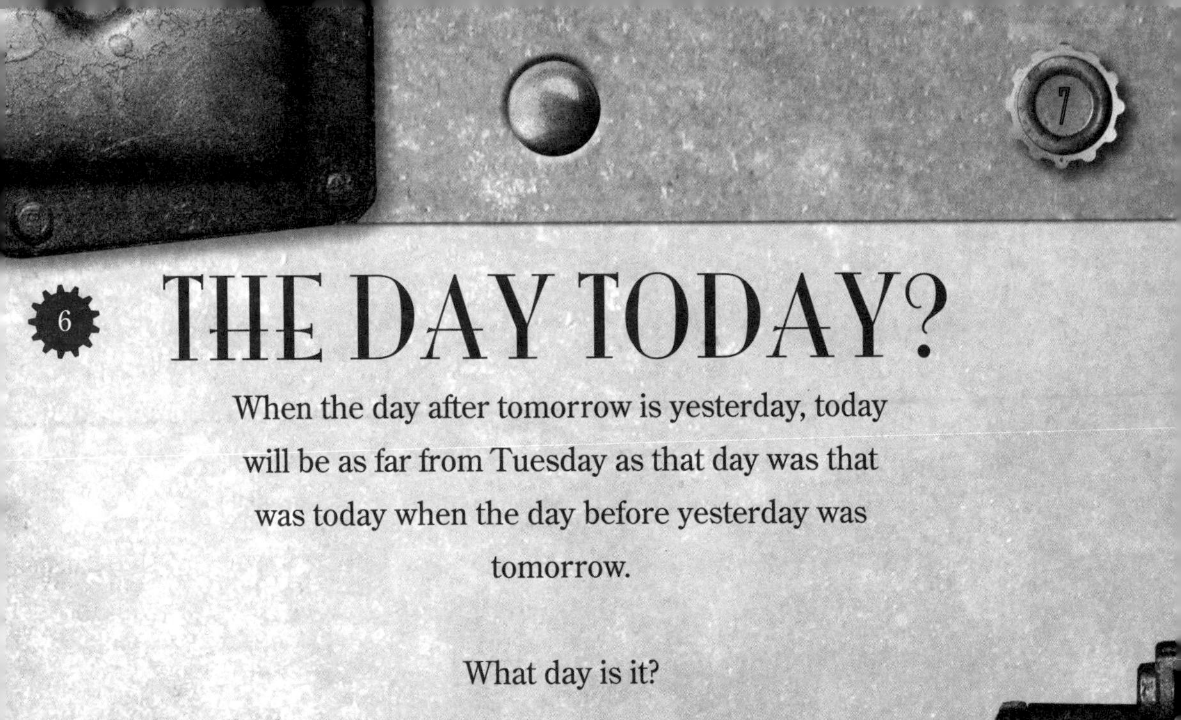

6 THE DAY TODAY?

When the day after tomorrow is yesterday, today will be as far from Tuesday as that day was that was today when the day before yesterday was tomorrow.

What day is it?

Solution on p. 175

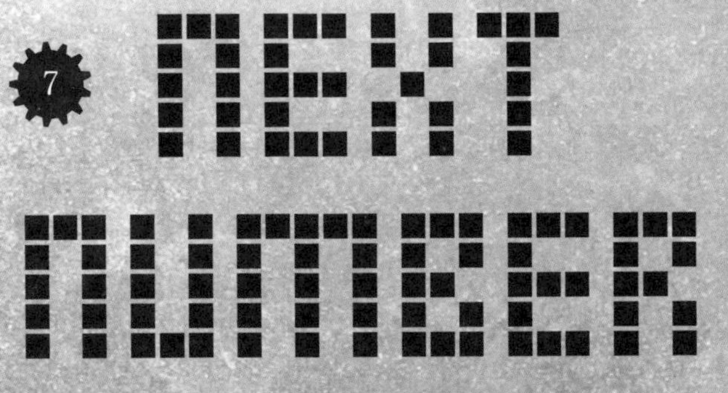

7 NEXT NUMBER

What is the next number in the sequence:

1, 3, 4, 7, 11, 18, ??

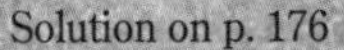

Solution on p. 176

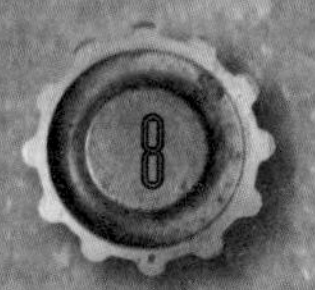

8 Three Squares

Make three squares by moving four matches.

Solution on p. 176

9 BOXED UP

Adam the sculptor has made a giant cube out of wooden boards measuring 6 feet by 6 feet. Adam can see all six sides of his cube from where he is standing. Where is Adam standing?

Solution on p. 176

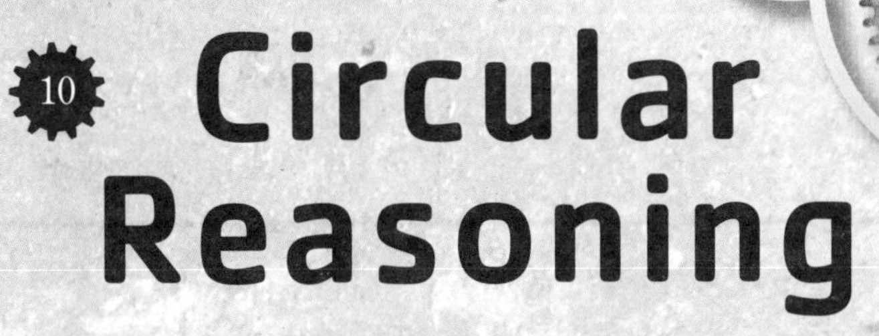

10 Circular Reasoning

How would you make a perfect circle using only these eight straight lines?

Solution on p. 176

11 Rising Tide

A boat floats in the harbor at low tide. A ladder is attached to the side of the boat, and five rungs of the ladder are showing above the waterline. If the rungs are 8 inches apart and the sea level rises at a rate of 13 inches per hour, how many rungs will be showing above water after two-and-a-half hours?

Solution on p. 176

12 DIOPHANTUS' EPITAPH

The gravestone of the Greek mathematician Diophantus
was said to have contained this riddle:
"God gave him his boyhood one-sixth of his life;
One-twelfth more as youth while whiskers grew rife;
And then yet one-seventh ere marriage begun.
In five years, there came a bouncing new son.
Alas, the dear child of master and sage
After attaining half the measure of his
father's life, chill fate took him.
After consoling his fate by the science of numbers
for four years, he reached the end of his life."

Can you figure out how old Diophantus was
when he died?

Solution on p. 176

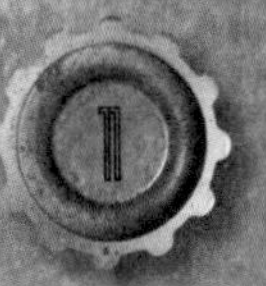

13 TRAIN DELAYS

The new train service from Santa Rosa to San Jose is 100 miles long. The advertised journey will be completed in 2 hours, making an average speed of 50 mph. If the train completes the first 50 miles at 25 mph, how fast will it have to go for the rest of the trip to make its average up to the required 50 miles per hour?

Solution on p. 177

14 Does This Add Up?

Replace the letters with numbers (0–9) to make this equation work (each letter represents a different number):

SEVEN + SEVEN + SIX = TWENTY

Solution on p. 177

15 String Trio

Three friends, James, Elizabeth, and Hannah, play in a chamber music group. Two out of the three play the violin, two play the viola, and two play the cello. The one who doesn't play the violin doesn't play the viola either. The one who doesn't play the viola doesn't play the cello.

Which instruments do they all play if James doesn't play the violin?

Solution on p. 177

16 Classroom Conundrum

Mrs. Rogers' elementary school class has just seven students this year. How can she arrange their desks so that there are six rows with three students sitting in each row?

Solution on p. 177

17 Equal Shares

Mrs. Brown is late getting to the store. She buys the last five apples in the produce section, but she has six children, herself, and a husband to feed. How does she share the fruit equally among all the family members?

Solution on p. 177

18 SUMMING UP

Move one match to make the sum correct.

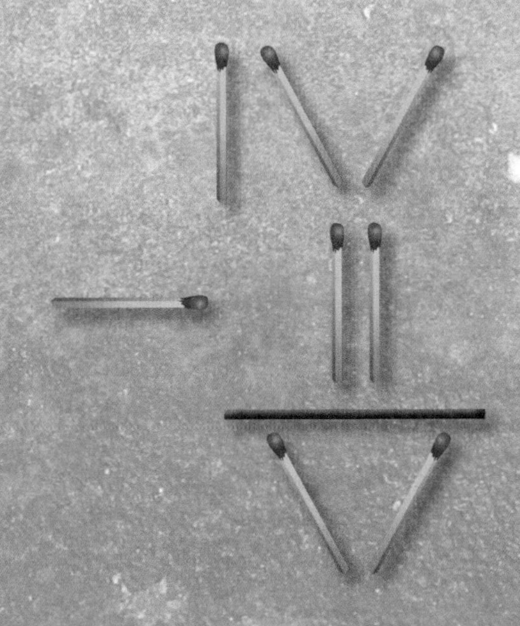

Solution on p. 177

19 MATCHING SOCKS

Bradley is a very untidy boy. In his sock drawer, his socks are all mixed together. There are 14 red socks, 10 purple socks, and 6 white socks. There has been a power outage and it is completely dark in his bedroom. What is the minimum number of socks that Bradley should take out of his drawer to be sure that he has at least two the same color?

Solution on p. 178

20 A LONG MULTIPLICATION

What is the value of the following product:

$$(x - a)\ (x - b)\ (x - c)\ \ldots\ (x - y)\ (x - z)$$

There are 26 parentheses, and the variables *a–z* can be any number.

Solution on p. 178

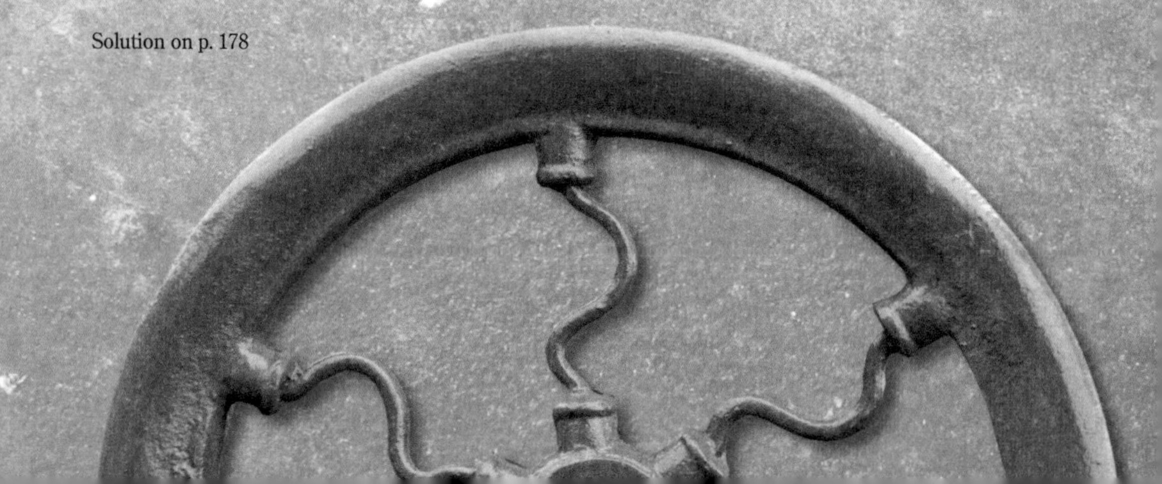

21 A Snail's Pace

A snail starts to climb a wall one morning. The wall is 10 feet high. The snail makes good progress during the day, climbing at a rate of 3 feet a day. However, it slips back 2 feet every night. How many days does the snail take to reach the top of the wall?

Solution on p. 178

22

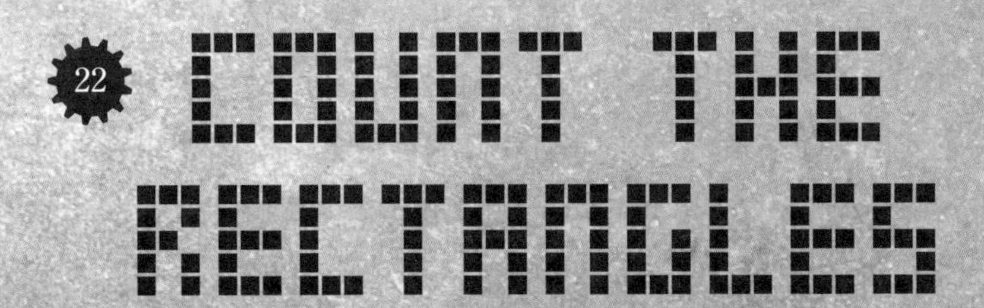

Professor Cordon is staring at his kitchen floor. How many different rectangles can he make out of the eight tiles?

Solution on p. 178

23 DRIP DROP

How many drops of wine can be put into an empty wine glass?

Solution on p. 178

24 TRIANGULATION

Can you help Clive the plumber? He needs to connect these six pipes to make three equilateral triangles.

Solution on p. 178

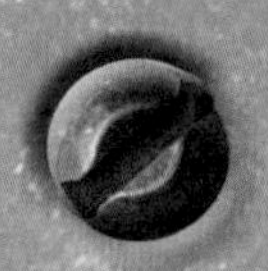

CHESS MATES

In the monthly tournament at the Checkmates Chess Club, the number of competitors varies month by month, but the principle is always the same: a direct knockout, and the loser of each game leaves the tournament. In the event of a draw, the player with the black pieces wins. Depending on the numbers, some competitors may be given byes through the early rounds.

There are 55 competitors in March's competition. How many individual games are there in the whole tournament?

Solution on p. 179

26 Archer's Score

Lily has set up an archery target in the backyard. How can she score exactly 100 firing at a board with the following scores? (She may use as many arrows as she likes.)

Solution on p. 179

27 The Monty Hall Problem

This famous puzzle stumped even mathematics professors. Can you get it right?

A game show contestant stands on stage in front of three closed doors, numbered 1, 2, and 3. The host tells her that behind two of the doors is a goat, but behind one of them is a brand new car. The contestant is asked to choose a door, and goes for door number 1. The host opens door number 3 to reveal that there is a goat standing behind it munching on some grass. He now gives the contestant a choice: she can stick with door number 1 or she can change to door number 2.

What should the contestant do to give her the best chance of winning the car?

Solution on p. 179

28 PAY RISE, PAY CUT

Stephen earned $1,224.45 per year two years ago.
His salary increased by $\frac{1}{4}$ last year, then fell by $\frac{1}{5}$ this year.

How much does he earn now?

Solution on p. 179

29 Equal Areas

These matches cover an area of 3 square matches. Can you move two matches and add two more, but keep the area they cover the same?

Solution on p. 179

30 DO RE MI

Replace the letters with numbers (0–9) to make these equations work (each letter represents a different number):

RE + MI = FA

DO + SI = MI

LA + SI = SOL

Solution on p. 179

31 SEPARATE SAMPLES

Dr. Mulligan needs to keep his samples separated in their tray to prevent contamination. He can use two square dividers, which may be any size. Where should he place the dividers?

Solution on p. 180

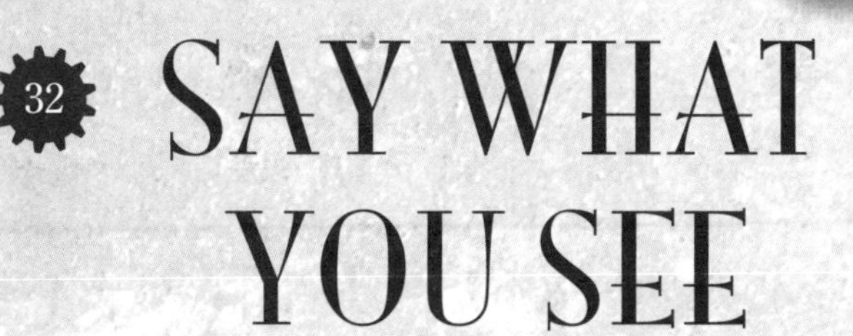

32 SAY WHAT YOU SEE

What is the next term in the series:

1
11
21
1211
111221
312211

Solution on p. 180

33 PICK UP STICKS

Professor Bell can only take one of his assistants—Alexander or Graham—to the science conference. To settle the matter, he proposes a game and lays 21 sticks on the table. Taking turns, Alexander and Graham may pick up one, two, or three sticks. Whoever picks up the final stick must stay at home and take care of the laboratory.

They toss a coin to see who goes first, and Graham is first to pick. Alexander smiles, because he knows he is going to the conference. How does Alexander make sure he wins?

Solution on p. 180

34 Matching Up

Move two matches to make this equation work.

Solution on p. 180

35 TOSS A COIN

Lucas cannot decide whether to go to the bar or to stay at home with his girlfriend. He decides to toss a coin to make his decision for him. He wants it to be equally likely that he will go to the bar as stay at home. However, he knows the only coin he has is biased, but doesn't know what the bias is. How can he use the biased coin to make his decision for him?

Solution on p. 180

36 RUNNING DOG

Michael, Amanda, and their dog Spike set out together for a walk. Michael walks at 4 mph, while Amanda lags behind, doing 3 mph. Spike, full of energy, runs back and forth between the two of them for the whole time at a speed of 8 mph. They walk for an hour like this. How far does Spike run in this time?

Solution on p. 181

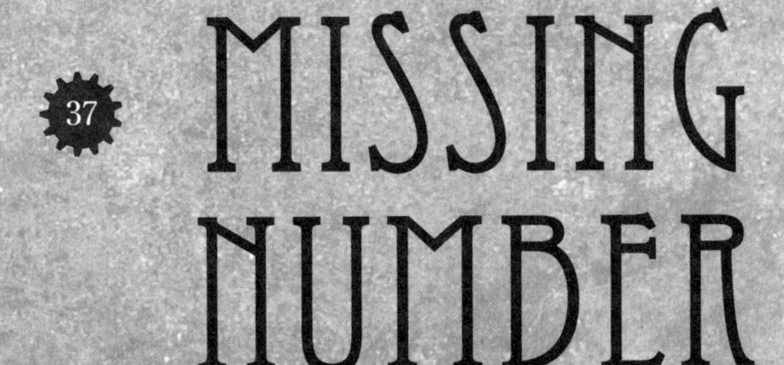

37 MISSING NUMBER

What is the next number in the following sequence:

7, 10, 8, 11, 9, 12, ??

Solution on p. 181

38 HOW LONG?

Which of the two horizontal lines is the longer?

Solution on p. 181

39 *Sunbathing Sea Lions*

Some sea lions are lying in the sun on two rocks in the harbor. The sea lions on the larger rock shout over to the sea lions on the smaller rock: "If one of you comes over here, there will be twice as many sea lions in our group as in yours." The sea lions on the smaller rock reply: "Well, if one of you comes over here, our numbers will be equal."

How many sea lions are there on each rock?

Solution on p. 181

40 LAWN MOWERS

Between them, it takes gardening duo Carter and Lewis eight days to mow all the lawns on their rounds, both working as fast as they can. On his own, Carter can mow the lawns in 12 days. How many days would it take Lewis to mow the lawns on his own?

Solution on p. 181

41 Two Triangles

Move two matches to make two triangles.

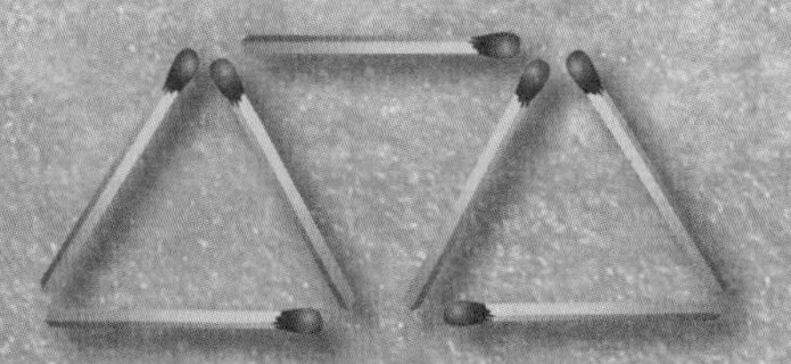

Solution on p. 181

42 EQUAL SHARES

Farmer Barnett wants to be scrupulously fair to his four sons when he retires. Can you divide his land into four parts so that each part is the same size and shape, and has the same number of fields and woods on it?

Solution on p. 181

43 Jealous Guys

Three men and their fiancées need to cross a river by boat. Their boat only takes two people at a time, but the men are very protective, and agree to the following rule (much to the bemusement of their fiancées, needless to say!): there must never be more men than women on either riverbank at any time, and the boat must have at least one person to row it.

How can our jealous guys achieve their aim?

Solution on p. 182

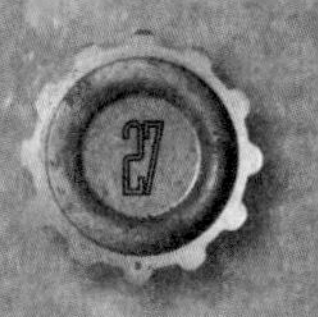

44 GWENDOLINE'S GRANDMA

Gwendoline tells her friends that her grandmother is only one year older than her mother.

How can that be?

Solution on p. 182

45 SHADOWY SECRET

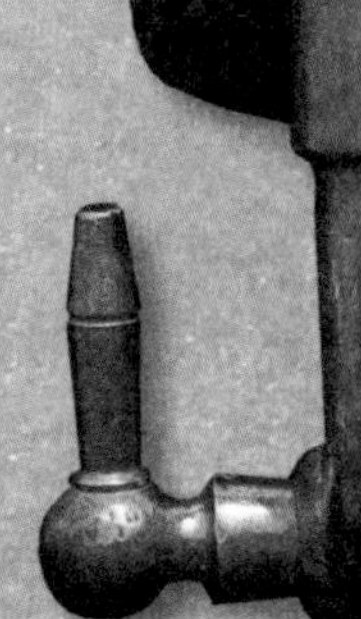

Which square is lighter, A or B?

Solution on p. 182

46 GEAR POWER

Stephenson is playing around with gear ratios for his new locomotive. He connects five gears in a row, the first connected to the second, the second to the third, and so on.

The second and fourth gears are twice the size of the first gear, the third gear is half the size of the first gear, while the fifth gear is the same size as the first gear. Stephenson gives the first gear one complete revolution.

How many times does the fifth gear turn?

Solution on p. 182

47 Gear Power II

If Stephenson turns the first gear in the above set of gears in a clockwise direction, what direction will the fourth gear turn in?

Solution on p. 182

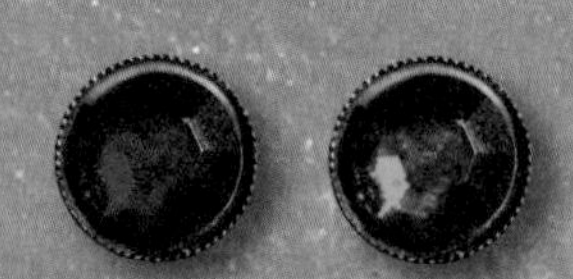

48 WHO'S WHO?

Three identical triplets, Anne, Beatrix, and Caroline, are visiting David's house for coffee. They are sitting in a line on the couch, and David wants to figure out which sister is which.

He knows that Anne always tells the truth, that Beatrix always lies, and that Caroline sometimes lies and sometimes tells the truth.

David asks the following questions.

He asks the sister on the left, "Who is sitting in the middle?"
She replies, "That's Anne."

He asks the sister in the middle, 'What is your name?'
She replies, "I'm Caroline."

He asks the sister on the right, "Who is sitting in the middle?"
She replies, "That's Beatrix."

David smiles. He now knows who is who.
How?

Solution on p. 182

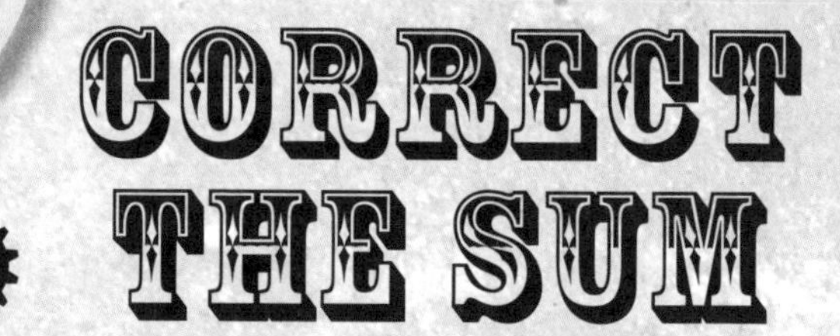

49 CORRECT THE SUM

Move two matches to make this sum correct.

Solution on p. 183

50 A KNOTTY PROBLEM

Maskelyne the magician stands on stage holding a piece of rope. He tells his audience that he can hold the rope with one end in each hand and tie a knot in it without letting go.

How does he do it?

Solution on p. 183

51 Bookworm

Dr. Rutherford keeps his ten-volume *Encyclopedia Britannica* on its own shelf in the library, stored in order from left to right with the spines facing outward. Each volume is 5 inches thick, including front and back covers that are each ½ inch thick.

Starting on page 1 of Volume 1, a bookworm eats its way in a straight line through the complete set, finishing on the last page of Volume 10.

What distance does the bookworm travel?

Solution on p. 183

52 CHEATING THE CHEATER

Gordon is anxious to join the Magic Circle, but he knows that the devious Lord Sleight, its President, has it in for him. He is told to attend a meeting of the Inner Circle, where he will be asked to draw one of two marbles from a bag.

One of the marbles will be white, the other black. If Gordon draws the white marble, he can join. If he draws the black marble, he will be excluded for life.

The night before the meeting, Gordon hears from his spies in the Circle that Lord Sleight is going to switch the marbles at the last minute and make them both black. What should Gordon do to make sure he can join?

Solution on p. 183

53

Replace the letters with numbers (0–9) to make this equation work (each letter represents a different number):

$$(AA)^B = ABBA$$

Solution on p. 183

54 SNOWED UNDER

It has been snowing heavily, and Mrs. Thomas looks out into her backyard. She sees that there is three times more snow in her backyard than that of her neighbor, Mrs. Brown. How can this be possible?

Solution on p. 183

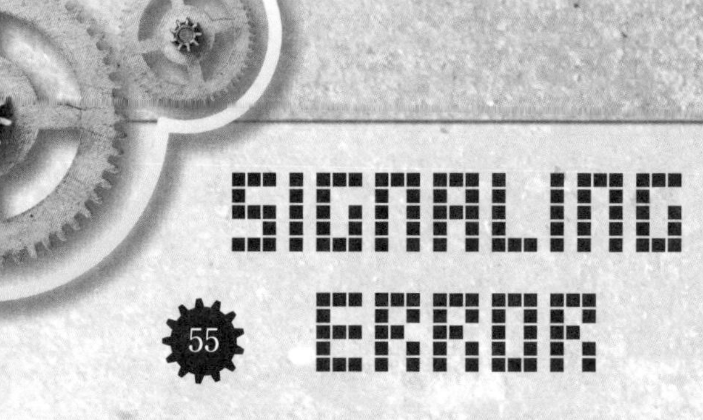

SIGNALING ERROR

55

Read this sign:

!

PLEASE
LEAVE YOUR
HATS, COATS,
AND BAGS AT
AT THE RECEPTION

Solution on p. 184

Now turn straight to the answer.

Hardware Store

Mr. Braithwaite is at the hardware store.

He asks: “What does one cost?”

“One dollar,” replies the salesperson.

“And 10?”

”Two dollars.”

”What about 310?”

”That will be three dollars.”

What is Mr. Braithwaite buying?

Solution on p. 184

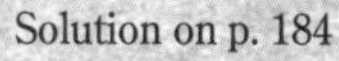

Three Squares

Move three matches to make three squares.

Solution on p. 184

58 Crescent Moon

This crescent moon is formed of two circles. C is the center of the larger circle. The width of the crescent between points B and D is 9 inches. Between points E and F, it is 5 inches. What are the diameters of the two circles?

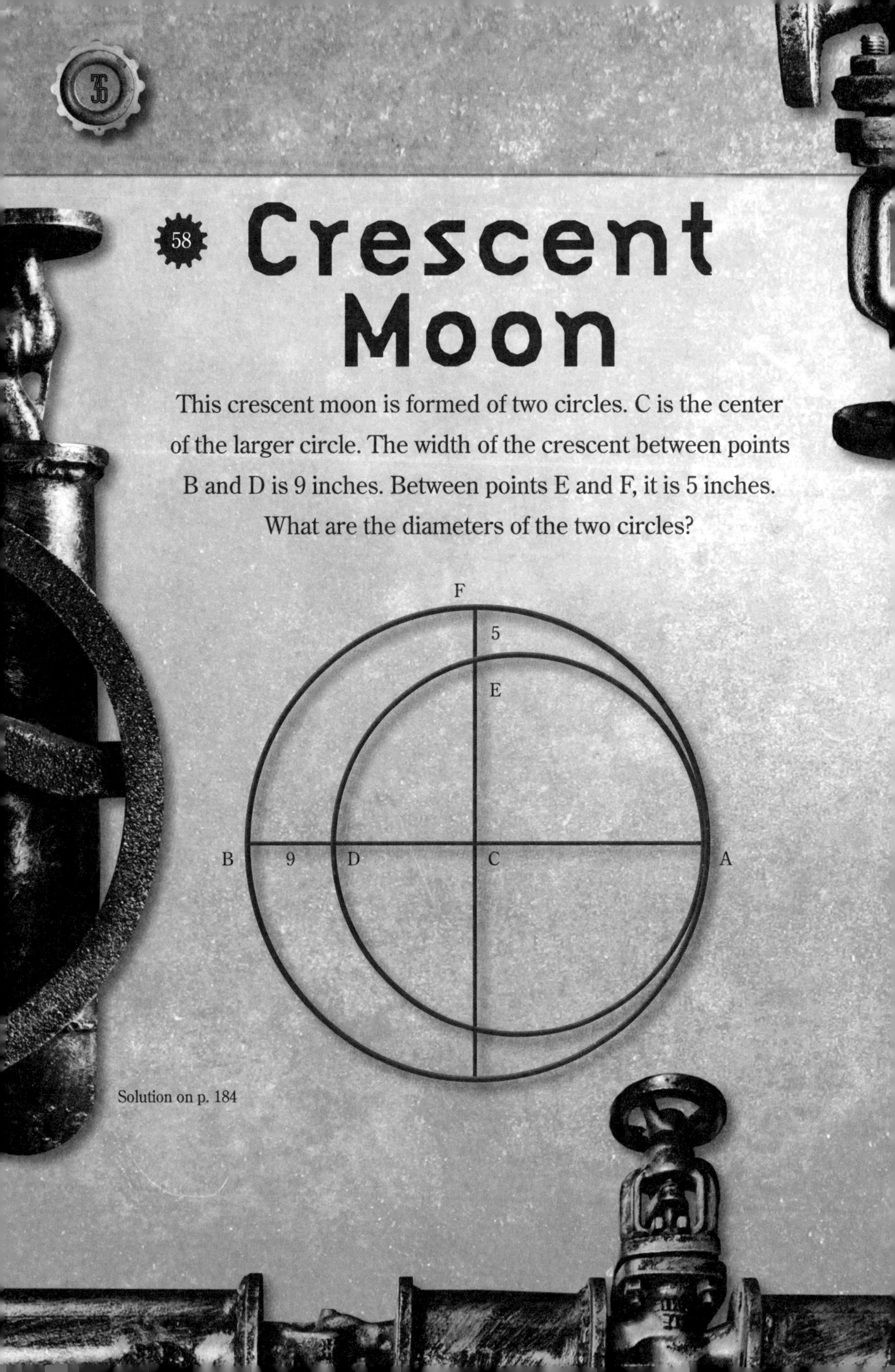

Solution on p. 184

59 FOUR GLASSES

Sitting at a table at a restaurant are a father, a mother, a son, a daughter, a brother, a sister, two cousins, an uncle, and an aunt. One of them goes to the bar to get a round of drinks. She comes back with four glasses of beer, but she has bought a drink for everyone. How?

Solution on p. 184

60 Pizza Deal

Mama's Pizzeria is offering a special deal this week. Buy any small 10-inch Margherita pizza and you get a second one half price. The 10-inch costs $7 and a larger 14-inch costs $10. Is their offer a good deal, or are you better off buying one 14-inch pizza instead?

Solution on p. 184

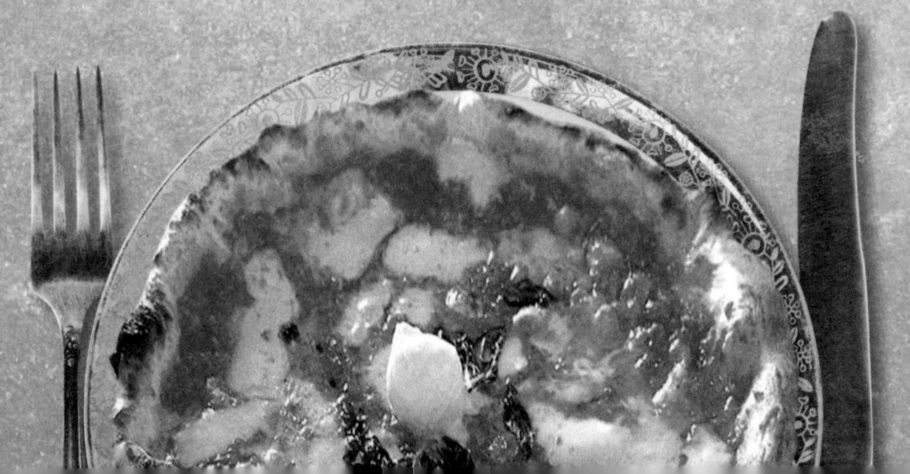

61 Four Rectangles

Move two matches to make four identical rectangles.

Solution on p. 185

62 A Perfect Egg

Mrs. Housman is very fussy about her eggs. She likes them hard-boiled for exactly 9 minutes. Her husband has two hourglasses, one measuring 7 minutes and the other 4 minutes. IIow can hc cook the eggs to his wife's satisfaction using just these hourglasses?

Solution on p. 185

63 MUNCH, MUNCH

Can you slice this square into four identical shapes, each with one caterpillar in it, plus a leaf for the caterpillar to munch on?

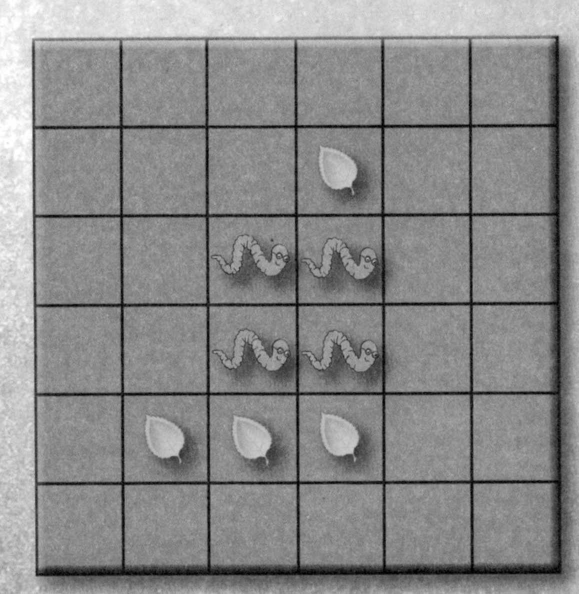

Solution on p. 185

64 Growth Spurt

Mrs. Morgan measures her son Malcolm's height with a mark on the wall. When Malcolm asks how tall he is, she replies, "You're 25 inches plus half your height."

How tall is Malcolm?

Solution on p. 185

65

A GRAINY PROBLEM

A poor farmer needs to go to the market to sell some grain and some lentils. He only has one sack to carry them in, but doesn't want to mix the grain with the lentils. He pours the grain in first, ties the middle of the sack, and fills the top half with the lentils. At the market, a brewer offers to buy the grain, but he has no use for the lentils. The brewer has his own sack to take the grain away in. The farmer wants to sell the brewer the grain, but needs to keep the lentils. They cannot cut either of the sacks, and they have to keep their own sacks. Pouring the grain and lentils anywhere on the ground would ruin them.

How does the farmer solve this conundrum?

Solution on p. 185

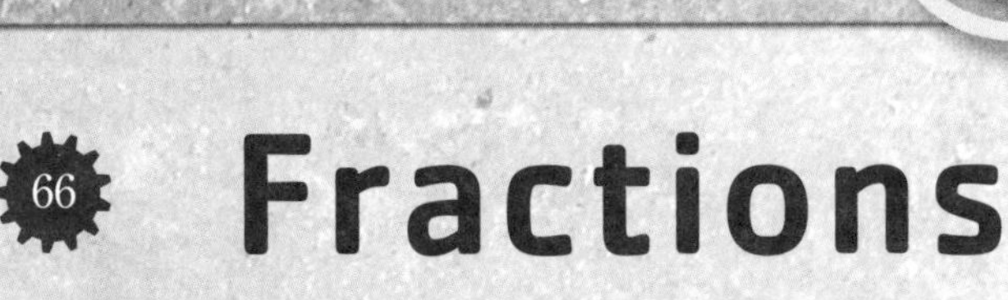

66 Fractions

65 percent can be written as the fraction $\frac{13}{20}$ (with the lowest possible denominator). How would you write $58\frac{1}{3}$ percent as a simplified fraction with the lowest possible denominator?

Solution on p. 185

67 Take Away a Square

Move three matches to turn these five squares into four.

Solution on p. 186

68 Magnetic Attractions

Faraday is standing in a room wearing nothing but his pajamas. The room is empty except for a wooden table with two iron rods placed on it. One of the rods is a magnet.

How does Faraday figure out which iron rod is the magnet?

Solution on p. 186

69 A LONG SUM

What is the sum of the first 100 whole numbers? That is:

1 + 2 + 3 ... + 99 + 100

(Clue: you do not need to add them all up.)

Solution on p. 186

70 Crippen's Cell

Dr. Crippen the murderer has been locked in a round cell. He has had all his possessions taken from him, except his pocket compass. Starting from the window of the cell, which is not facing due south, Crippen takes three paces due north, where he reaches the wall of the cell. He then turns 90 degrees and takes four paces due west before reaching the wall again.

How many paces is the diameter of Dr. Crippen's cell?

Solution on p. 186

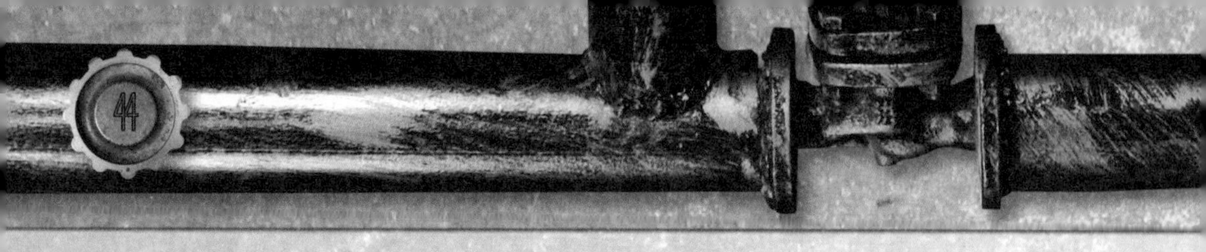

71 Eight Triangles

Arrange these six matches to
form eight equilateral triangles.

Solution on p. 186

72 A Grave Problem

Thomas the grave digger sits down for a well-earned rest.
He has just dug a grave 7 feet long, 2 feet wide,
and 6 feet deep.

Can you calculate how much earth there is in the grave?

Solution on p. 187

73 TURNING CARDS

Can you turn all four of these playing cards upside down by turning three at a time?

What is the minimum number of turns you can do it in?

Solution on p. 187

74 MISSING NUMBER

What is the missing number in this series?

??, 49, 2,401, 5,764,801

Solution on p. 187

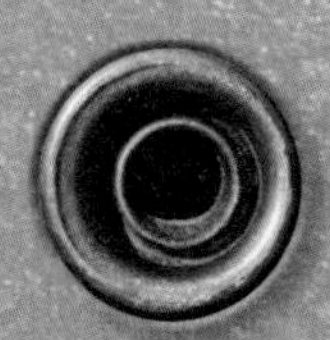

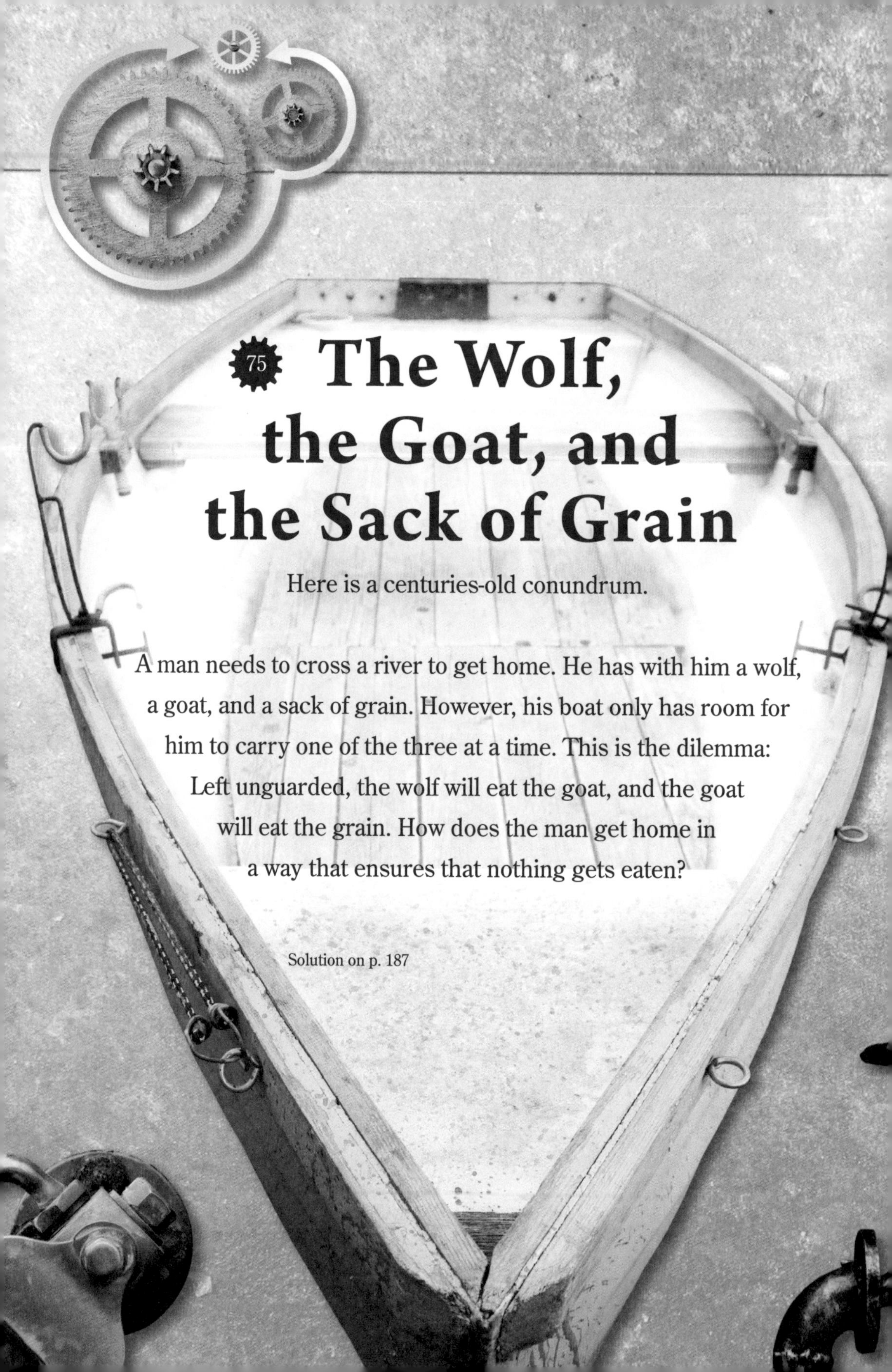

75 The Wolf, the Goat, and the Sack of Grain

Here is a centuries-old conundrum.

A man needs to cross a river to get home. He has with him a wolf, a goat, and a sack of grain. However, his boat only has room for him to carry one of the three at a time. This is the dilemma: Left unguarded, the wolf will eat the goat, and the goat will eat the grain. How does the man get home in a way that ensures that nothing gets eaten?

Solution on p. 187

76 FIVE SQUARES

Move two matches to make five squares all the same size.

Solution on p. 187

77 FIGURE EIGHT

Marie is numbering her laboratory log book by hand.
The book has 100 pages, so she numbers them from 1 to 100.

How many times will she write the figure 8?

Solution on p. 187

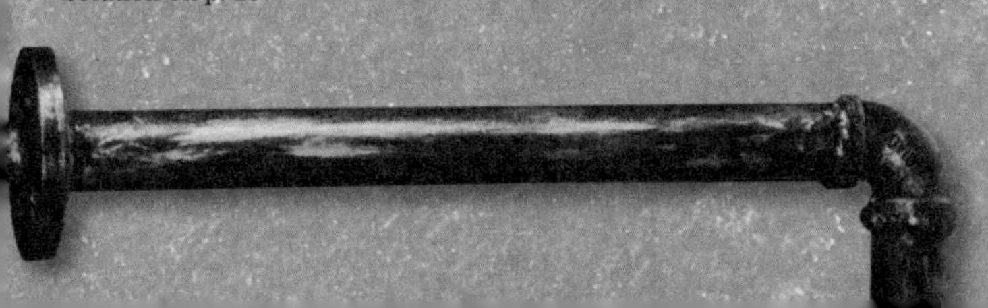

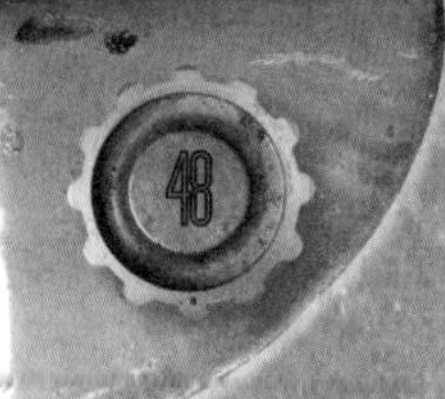

78 The Mountaineer

Mummery the mountaineer sets out at 5 a.m. to climb Mount Rainier. He reaches the summit at noon, and stays there for the rest of the day and night staring at the stars. The following morning, he starts his descent at 5 a.m. and, retracing his steps, he arrives back in town at 10 a.m. Did Mummery find himself at any point along his route at the same place and the same time on both days?

Solution on p. 187

79 *Parallel Thinking*

Are these lines parallel, or are they sloping toward each other?

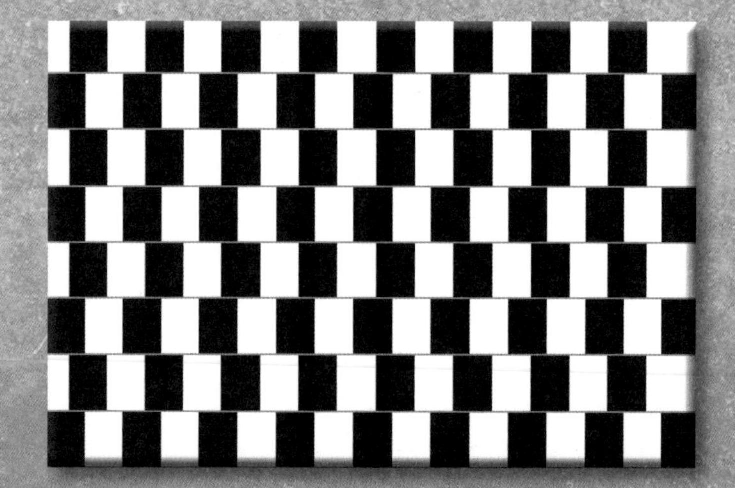

Solution on p. 188

80 NORTH FACING

The four sides of a house all face due north.
Where is the house?

Solution on p. 188

81 THE KANGAROO AND THE WALLABY

A kangaroo and a wallaby are set in a race against each other. From the starting line, they gallop to a pole 100 feet away, then turn immediately and come back again. The kangaroo covers 3 feet with each hop, and the wallaby 2 feet. The wallaby makes three hops for every two hops of the kangaroo.

Which marsupial will win?

Solution on p. 188

82 THE CARPENTER'S PROBLEM

A carpenter wants to make a square tabletop from this piece of wood. The tabletop needs to be as large as possible and made from as few pieces as possible. How many pieces will the carpenter need to cut the wood into?

Solution on p. 188

DOODLE FUN

Bored in class, Joseph draws on his notebook. How many squares can you count in Joseph's geometric doodle?

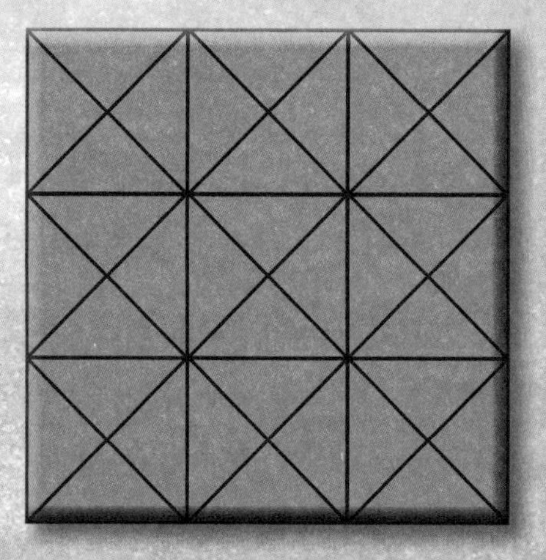

Solution on p. 188

84 Watch the Cards

Geraldine lays down four cards in front of her, side by side. The cards are numbered 2 to 5. She wants to rearrange the cards so that they are in ascending order from her left to her right. John is sitting opposite Geraldine and watches her take the card on John's left and move it to the other end. She then takes the third card from John's right and puts it to the end on the left from John's perspective.

What was the original order of the cards?

Solution on p. 188

85 FIVE MOVES

Move five matches to make five triangles.

Solution on p. 189

86 Who's the Grandpa?

Harvey is the son of Mary. Mary is the sister of Martin. Patrick is the brother of Harvey. Theresa is the daughter of Martin. Martin is the son of Elijah.

Who is Patrick's grandfather?

Solution on p. 189

87 Black and White

In this grid, there are white and black checkers pieces. The horizontal rows are labeled 1–4 and the vertical columns are labeled A–D. Each piece is the opposite color on its reverse side, so turning it over changes its color.

Choosing one row or column at a time and turning over all four pieces in that line in one turn, what is the minimum number of turns you would need to turn all the checkers black?

Solution on p. 189

88 Think Laterally

Move one match to make the scales balance.

(The answer is sneaky!)

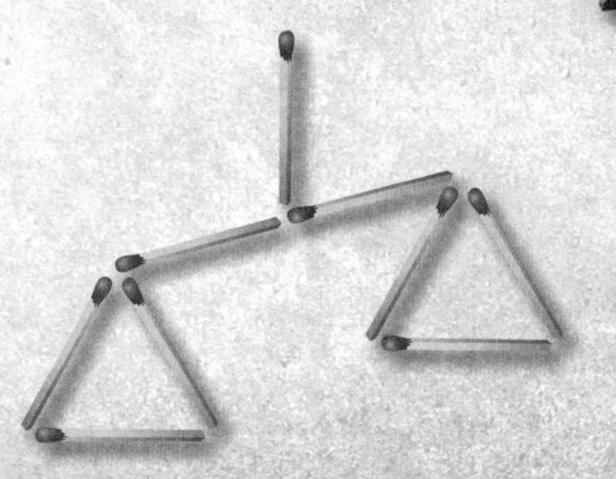

Solution on p. 189

89 WAR AND PEACE

How would you balance a copy of Tolstoy's epic novel, *War and Peace*, all 1,000 pages of it, on a single piece of paper?

Solution on p. 189

90 PICKY PROBLEM

Arrange 13 toothpicks to make the following incorrect equation:

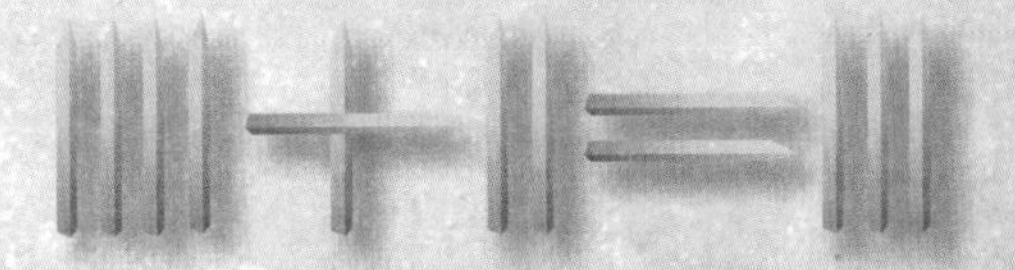

Now move one toothpick to make the equation correct. (You are not allowed to change the = sign!)

Solution on p. 189

91 Trouble at the Mill

Mrs. Herman is boasting again. Invited to dinner at the Riveras', she declares, "One hundred and fifty people work at my husband's mill." Mrs. Rivera's troublesome daughter Rose disagrees. "I know there are not that many," she says. Her son Reginald, always the peacemaker, says, "Well, I'm sure there is at least one worker at the mill." All this time, Mr. Herman is squirming in his seat. He knows that only one of them is right.

How many workers are there at Mr. Herman's mill?

Solution on p. 190

92 Half a Dozen

Here are 14 matches.

How would you take away seven to leave a dozen?

Solution on p. 190

93 Taking Stock

Dr. Watson is doing a stocktaking. At the start of the year, his bottle of rubbing alcohol was full and weighed 5 pounds. Now it is half full and weighs 3 pounds.

How much does the empty bottle weigh?

Solution on p. 190

94 Add a Line

By adding one straight line, can you make the following equation add up?

5+5+5=550

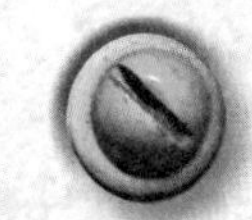

Solution on p. 190

95 Reckless Driving

Daimler is out driving his new car, and the car's lights have stopped working again. Nonetheless, he continues driving at high speed. There are no streetlights to show him the way and there is no moonlight. A woman dressed from head to toe in black steps out into the road. Despite all this, Daimler sees the woman, brakes, and manages to stop the car before he runs her over.

How was this possible?

Solution on p. 190

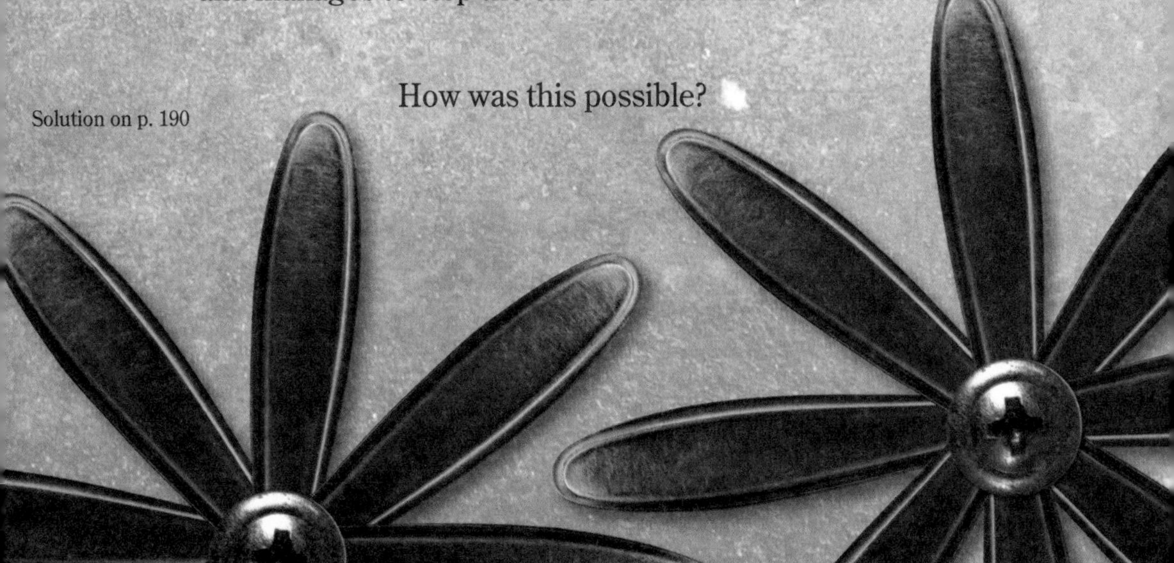

96 BET YOUR HOUSE

Two notoriously unlucky gamblers are in trouble with their bookmaker. Both have run up debts they cannot pay. The bookmaker asks the men if they would like to take on one final bet. They will both be sitting down facing each other, and the bookmaker will place a hat on their heads. Their hats will be either black or red, and both hats may be the same color. The men will be able to see each other's hat but not their own. If at least one of them can immediately guess correctly the color of his own hat, both will be let off their debts. But if they both guess wrongly, they will both lose their houses, and most likely their jobs and families. The bookmaker warns them that if he sees them giving any signals, they will lose their houses and he will break their legs! The two men consult. Has their luck just changed?

What would you advise them to do?

Solution on p. 190

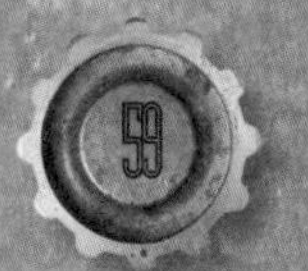

97 Four Triangles

Remove four matches to leave four identical triangles.

Solution on p. 191

CROSSING PATHS

Abigail and Agnes have mixed up their diaries. Abigail thinks she is visiting Agnes today, while Agnes thinks she is visiting Abigail. They both set off on foot for each other's house at 11 a.m. Abigail walks at 3 mph. Agnes ambles along at 2 mph. Which of the two is closer to Abigail's house when they meet each other on the road?

Solution on p. 191

Figure This Out

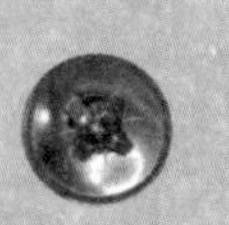

Adding the figures in the number 14, you get 5 (1 + 4).

Adding the figures of 58, you get 13 (5 + 8).

What is the smallest number whose figures add up to 29?

Solution on p. 191

Animal Magic

How many animals can you see in this picture?

Solution on p. 191

101 A Toast

Priscilla the singing telegram has an unusual job tonight. She is hiding inside a giant cake waiting to give a birthday boy a big surprise. Her cue to burst out of the cake and into song will be just after they have finished making a toast to the future. Priscilla listens as the toast is proposed. She waits for the guests all to clink their glasses. She counts exactly 55 clinks of crystal, and jumps out of the cake.

How many people were at the party?

Solution on p. 191

102 TRUTH OR LIE

Bill says to Martha:
"I always lie."

Is Bill lying or is he telling the truth?

Solution on p. 191

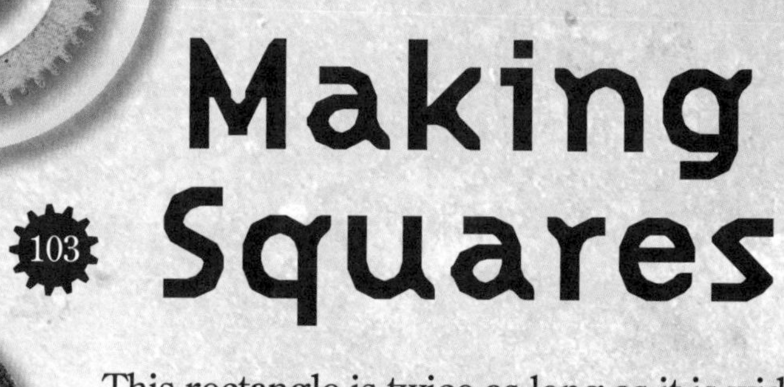

103 Making Squares

This rectangle is twice as long as it is wide. How would you cut it up so that you could rearrange the pieces into a square?

Solution on p. 192

104 Making Squares II

Now try something a little harder.
This rectangle is five times as long as it is square.
Can you cut it up and rearrange it into a square?

Solution on p. 192

105 Changing Places

This clock shows the time as a little more than 18 minutes to five. The hands will point at exactly the same places a little after 23 minutes after eight, but the hour hand and the minute hand will have changed places. How many pairs of times are there when the hands of a clock change places between 3 p.m. and midnight?

Solution on p. 192

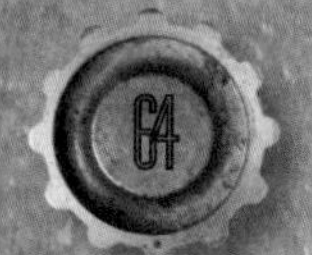

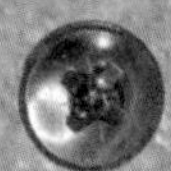

106 STRANGE HALVES

If 4 is half of 9, 6 is half of 11,
and 7 is half of 12, what is half of 13?

Solution on p. 193

107 SIX SQUARES

Move three matches to make six squares.

Solution on p. 193

108 Money Bags

Tyler is on his way to the fair with 139 dimes. He wants to bag his coins up in such a way that he can pay any amount between 1 and 139 by handing over a combination of bags without looking inside them.

What is the minimum number of bags Tyler will need.

Solution on p. 193

109 Up to a Hundred

Insert a mathematical symbol between each number so that the total comes to 100 (you'll also need a pair of parentheses):

1?2?3?4?5?6?7?8?9 = 100

Solution on p. 193

110

Heads and Feet

Mrs. Owen keeps chickens and pigs in her backyard. Between them, her animals have 9 heads and 30 feet.

How many pigs does Mrs. Owen have, and how many chickens?

Solution on p. 193

111

Weigh Anchor

Clive has taken Mathilda out for a romantic boat trip on the lake. They want to devote their attention to each other, so they drop the anchor out of the boat to stay put for an hour or so. Does the water level of the lake go up, go down, or stay the same when they do this?

Solution on p. 193

112 Three Squares

Move four matches to make three squares.

Solution on p. 194

113 COG COGITATION

Michael needs eight cogs for his new threshing machine as soon as possible. There are two metalworkers in town. Mr. Black tells him he can make one cog per week. Mr. Smith tells him he can manage three cogs per week. They will both charge him $1 per cog. When is the earliest he can have his 8 cogs?

Solution on p. 194

114 OLYMPIC MEDALIST

In the 10,000-meter final at the Olympics, Reinhard passed the runner in second place on the penultimate lap. Then Reinhard himself was passed by two runners on the finishing straight. What medal did Reinhard win?

Solution on p. 194

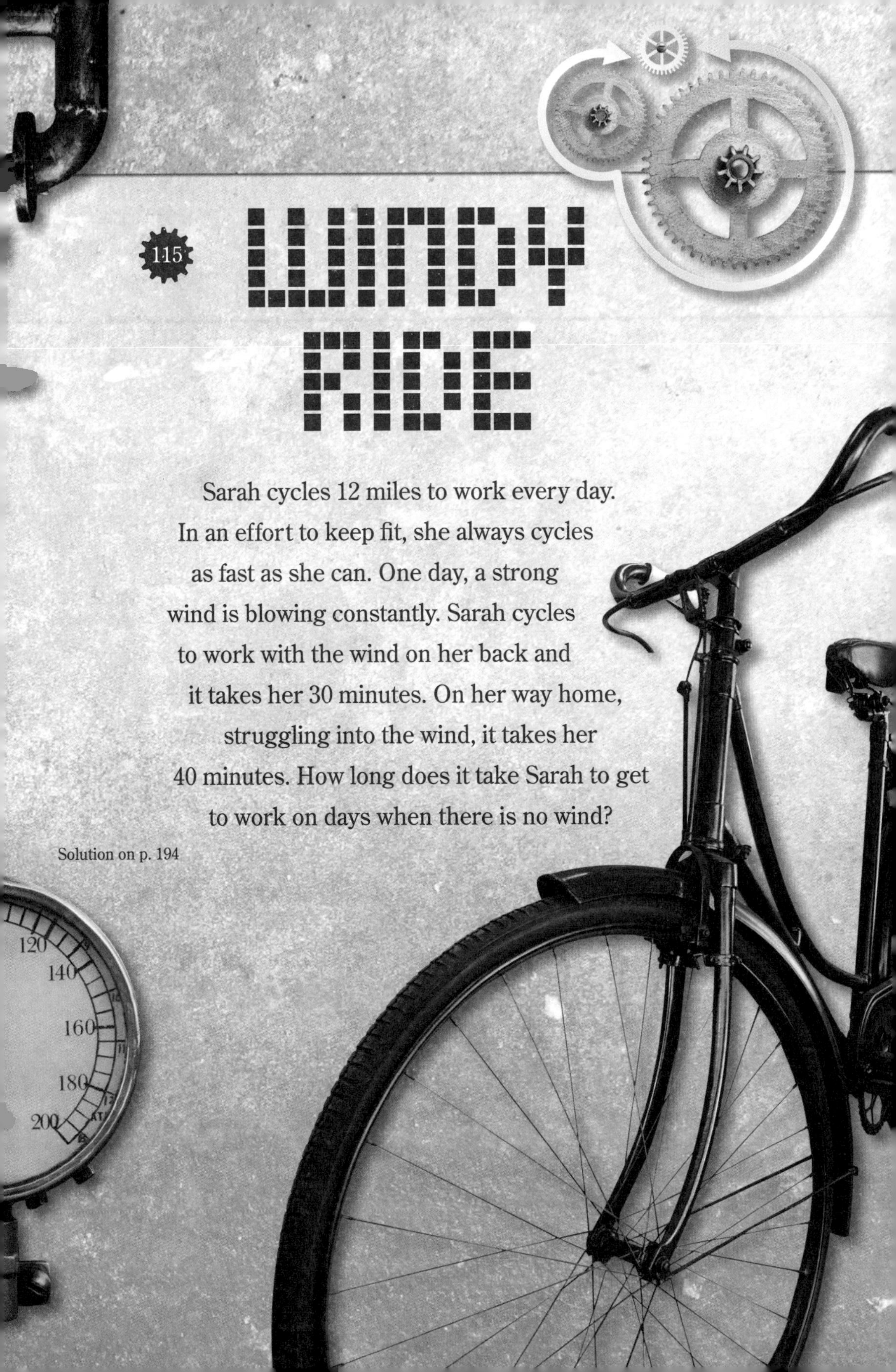

115

WINDY RIDE

Sarah cycles 12 miles to work every day. In an effort to keep fit, she always cycles as fast as she can. One day, a strong wind is blowing constantly. Sarah cycles to work with the wind on her back and it takes her 30 minutes. On her way home, struggling into the wind, it takes her 40 minutes. How long does it take Sarah to get to work on days when there is no wind?

Solution on p. 194

116

DAILY BREAD

Mrs. Maxwell needs to bake her bread for exactly 45 minutes. However, all she has are two wicks and a box of matches to keep track of time. She knows that both wicks take exactly one hour to burn all the way down, but she also knows that they burn at irregular rates—in other words, after half an hour, perhaps only one-third of the wick will have burned.

How does Mrs. Maxwell bake a perfect loaf?

Solution on p. 195

117 ODD AND EVEN

George and Arthur played seven games of badminton on Monday. Each won the same number of games as the other, and no game of badminton can end in a draw.

How did this happen?

Solution on p. 195

PRICING MIX

Mrs. Smith and Mrs. Bramley each sell apples at the market. Mrs. Smith sells her apples at three for a cent, Mrs. Bramley hers at two for a cent. At the end of the day, they both have 30 apples left and Mrs. Bramley has to go home. Mrs. Smith agrees to sell the rest of Mrs. Bramley's apples for her. To make things easier, Mrs. Smith mixes the apples together and sells them at a price of five for two cents.

Mrs. Smith is going to lose money on this deal. Why?

Solution on p. 195

119 POWER UP

Replace the letters with numbers to make the following true (each letter represents a different number):

$$B^{C} = CLIMB$$

Solution on p. 195

120 LOSE A SQUARE

Turn these five squares into four by moving two matches.

Solution on p. 195

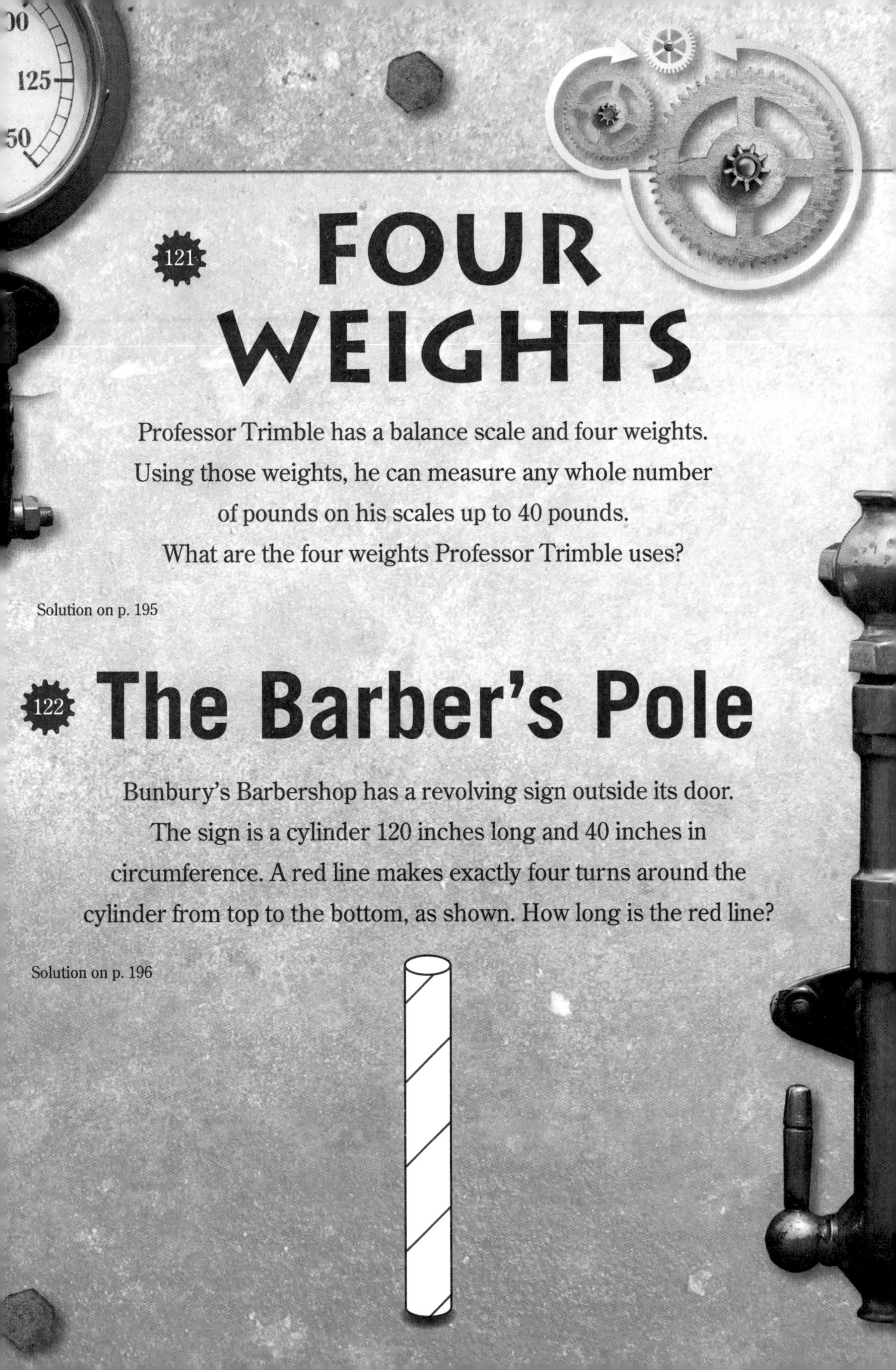

121

FOUR WEIGHTS

Professor Trimble has a balance scale and four weights. Using those weights, he can measure any whole number of pounds on his scales up to 40 pounds. What are the four weights Professor Trimble uses?

Solution on p. 195

122

The Barber's Pole

Bunbury's Barbershop has a revolving sign outside its door. The sign is a cylinder 120 inches long and 40 inches in circumference. A red line makes exactly four turns around the cylinder from top to the bottom, as shown. How long is the red line?

Solution on p. 196

123 CAT TIMES CAT

Replace the letters with numbers (0–9)
to make the equation work (each letter
represents a different number):

CAT = (C + A + T) x C x A x T

Solution on p. 196

124 BULBS IN THE BASEMENT

Patricia is feeling weak today, and doesn't want to climb any more stairs than she has to. There are three lights in her basement, each controlled by a switch on the first floor. How can Patricia figure out which switch controls which bulb by making just one trip down to the basement?

Solution on p. 196

BOY AND GIRL

A boy and a girl sit next to each other in class. "I am a boy," says the child with blue eyes. "I am a girl," says the child with brown eyes. Their teacher knows that at least one of them is lying. Which is the boy and which is the girl?

Solution on p. 196

126 NINE SQUARES

Move eight matches to make nine squares.

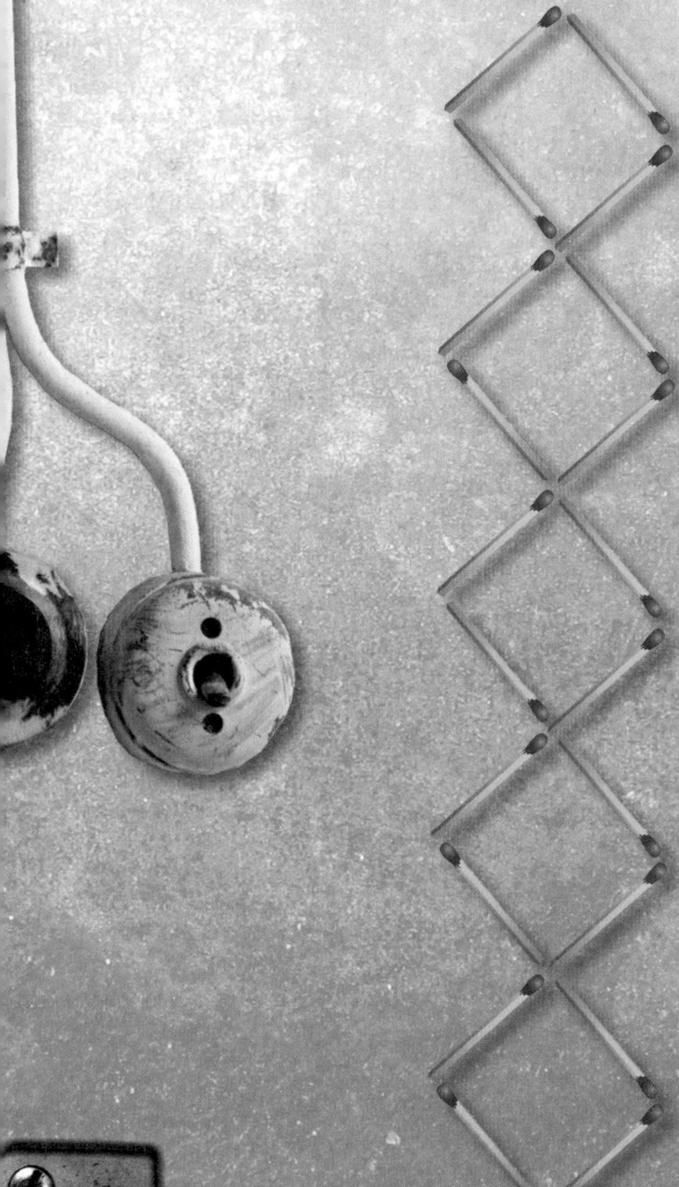

Solution on p. 196

127 A KING'S DILEMMA

A prisoner is brought before a bloodthirsty king and told he is to be executed at dawn. The king tells him, "You must make a statement. If I deem that statement to be true, you will be hanged. If I deem it to be false, you will face the firing squad."

The prisoner makes his statement, and the king decides he has to let him go.

What did the prisoner say?

Solution on p. 197

128 Sum to 1,000

How would you make 1,000 using only the figure 8 and the mathematical operation addition?

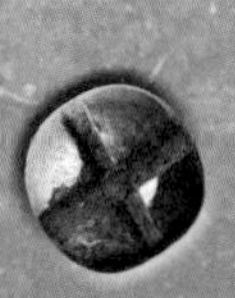

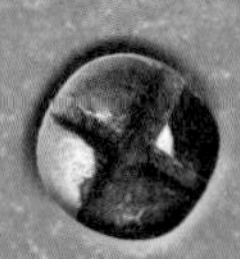

Solution on p. 197

129 Census Time

A census taker asks Mr. Smith at the doorway to his house:
"How many children do you have, and what are their ages?"
Mr. Smith replies:
"I have three daughters. If you multiply their ages together, you get the number of the house next door."

The census taker goes next door to number 36, but comes back a moment later and tells Mr. Smith that she needs more information. Mr. Smith replies, agitated, "I have to go now. My eldest child is calling me."

The census taker thanks Mr. Smith. She now knows the ages of his daughters.

How old are Mr. Smith's daughters?

Solution on p. 197

130 BETWEEN 4 AND 9

What mathematical symbol can you place between 4 and 9 to produce a number that is bigger than 4 but smaller than 9?

Solution on p. 197

131 THREE SHIRTS

Three friends, Mr. Red, Mr. Blue, and Mr. Black, meet for dinner. One man is wearing a red shirt, the second a blue shirt, and the third a black shirt. One of the friends remarks, "Have you noticed how we're all wearing shirts of a different color from our names?"

The man in the black shirt replies, "Yes, Mr. Blue, you're so right!"

Which man is wearing which shirt?

Solution on p. 197

132 NAILED ON

A carpenter attaches a square metal plate measuring 48 inches by 48 inches to a wooden board in such a way that there are 25 nails on each side of the square. Each nail is the same distance from its neighbors.

How many nails does the carpenter use?

Solution on p. 197

133 Matching Sum

Can you correct this equation by moving just one match?

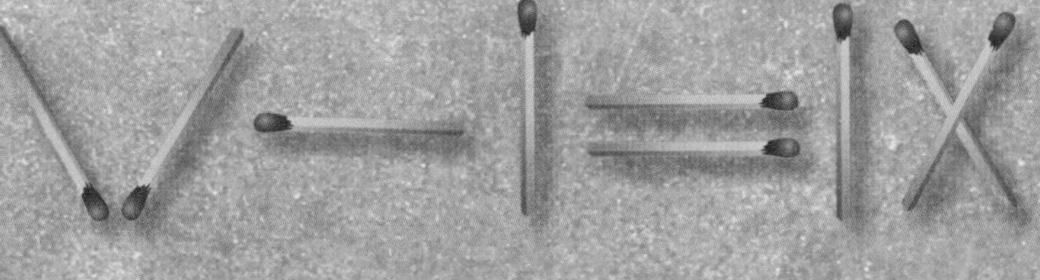

Solution on p. 197

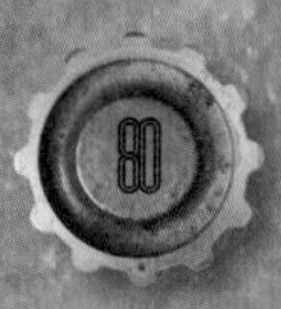

134 SOCCER LEAGUE

The soccer teams in the New York Senior League play each of the other teams once at home and once away in a full League season. There are 56 matches in total during the season.

How many teams are there in the New York Senior League?

Solution on p. 198

135 Door to Freedom

A man is imprisoned in a cell with two doors. The doors are unlocked, but a guard stands in front of each of them. The prisoner knows that one door leads to freedom, while the other leads to the dungeon and a lifetime of imprisonment. He can leave the cell and go through either door, but he cannot then turn back. One of the guards always tells the truth, while the other always lies. The man is allowed to ask one guard one question, but is not allowed to ask which one is the liar.

What question should he ask to secure his freedom?

Solution on p. 198

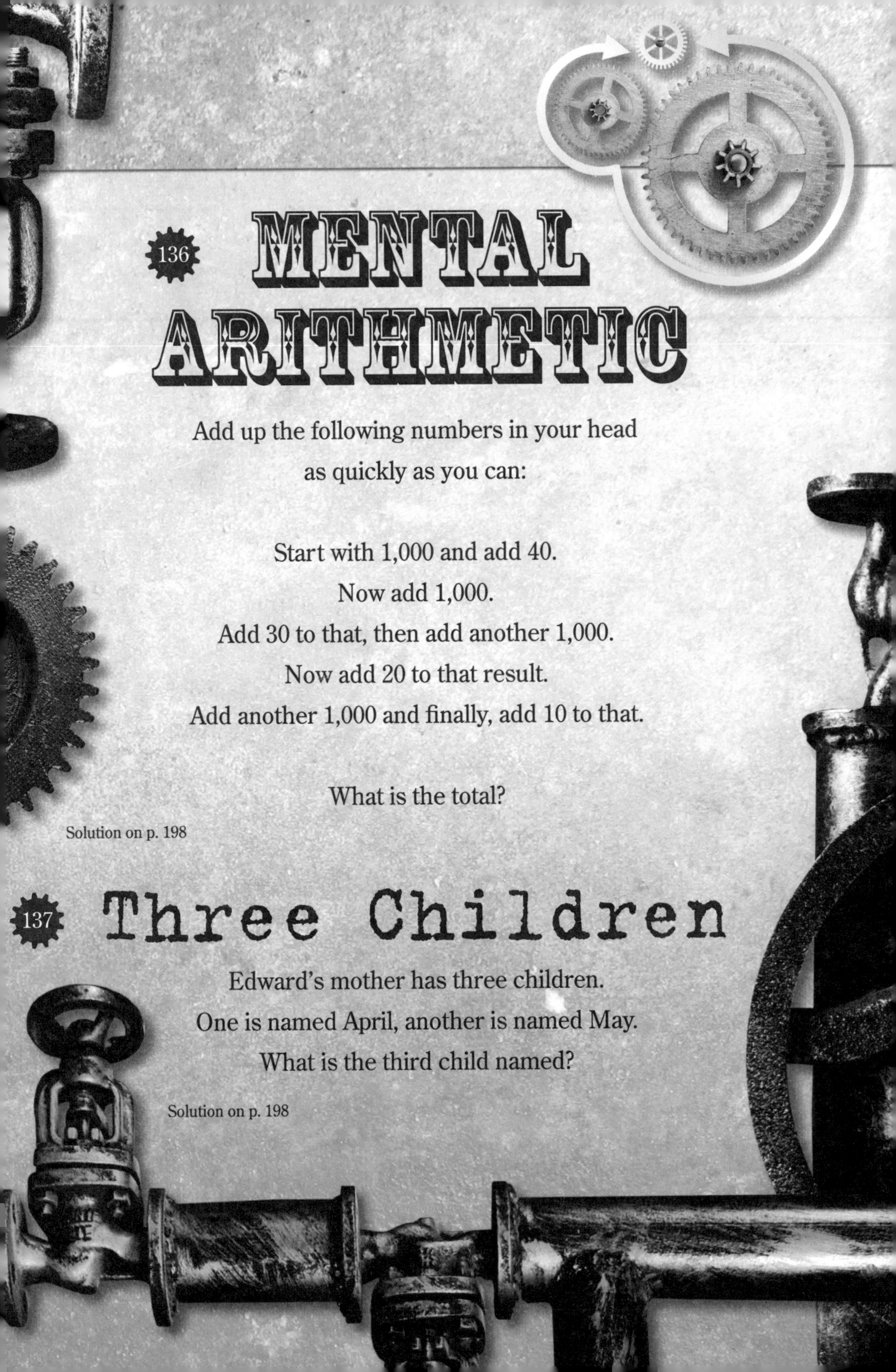

136 MENTAL ARITHMETIC

Add up the following numbers in your head
as quickly as you can:

Start with 1,000 and add 40.
Now add 1,000.
Add 30 to that, then add another 1,000.
Now add 20 to that result.
Add another 1,000 and finally, add 10 to that.

What is the total?

Solution on p. 198

137 Three Children

Edward's mother has three children.
One is named April, another is named May.
What is the third child named?

Solution on p. 198

138 FRANKENSTEIN'S BLOOD

Dr. Frankenstein is measuring out some blood for his monster. He has a large flask filled with blood that has a capacity of 8 pints (flask C), and two empty flasks with capacities of 3 and 5 pints, respectively (flasks A and B).

How can he measure exactly 4 pints of blood?

Solution on p. 198

A 3

B 5

C 8

139 Six Triangles

Remove three matches to leave six identical triangles.

Solution on p. 198

140 ISLAND OF FIRE

A man is stranded on an island covered with woods and surrounded by cliffs. One day, disaster strikes and a fire starts on the west end of the island. The wind is blowing from the west, and soon the whole island will be burned, killing everything in its path. The man cannot put out the fire, so how does he survive it?

Solution on p. 199

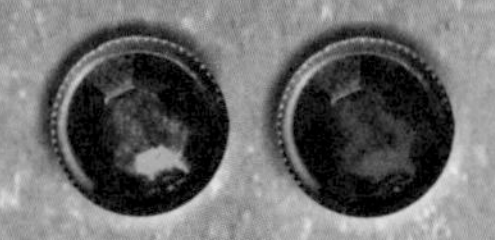

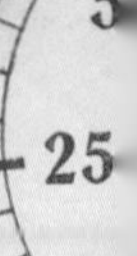

141 CIRCULAR ROOF

If the blue rectangle in the corner of the observatory measures 6 feet by 12 feet, what is the diameter of its circular roof?

Solution on p. 199

142 Class Treat

Mrs. Jenkins has brought a bag of candy into her class. There are 24 children in her class and 24 pieces of candy in the bag. The children all want a piece, but they also want Mrs. Jenkins to leave at least one piece of candy in the bag. How does she keep her class happy?

Solution on p. 199

143 Next Number

What is the next number in the sequence:

0, 1, 1, 2, 3, 5, 8, 13, 21, ??

Solution on p. 199

144 Three Figures

Which of these three figures is the largest?

Solution on p. 199

145 Appearing Area

Both these figures are made of the same four parts.
So where has the extra area marked "A" come from?

Solution on p. 200

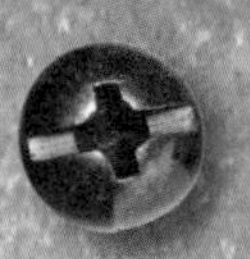

146 Nine Triangles

Draw three straight lines on this figure to make nine triangles.

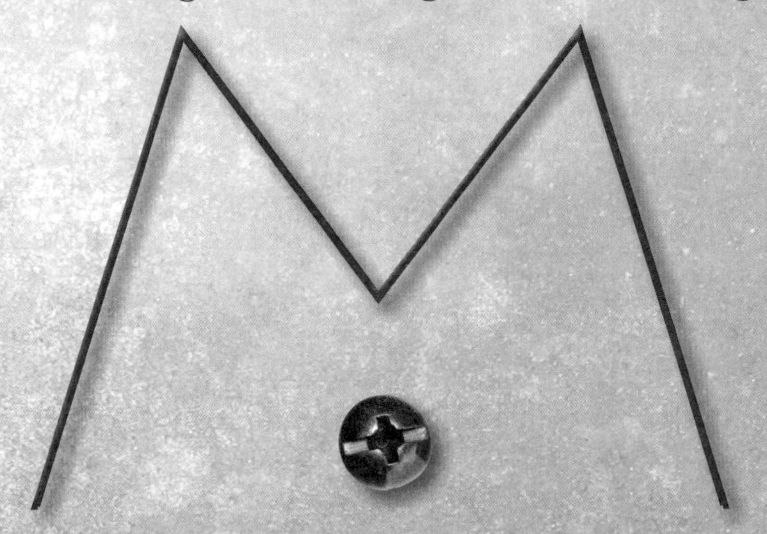

Solution on p. 200

147 CHOCOLATE SQUARES

Arnold has a bar of chocolate that is eight squares long and four squares wide. How many times does he have to break the chocolate so that all the squares are separate pieces? (He can only break one piece of chocolate at a time, and must break it horizontally or vertically.)

Solution on p. 200

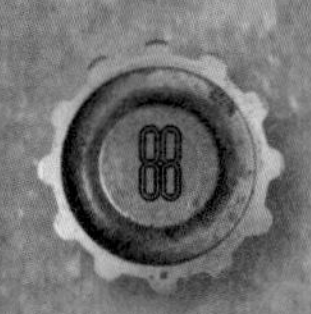

AROUND THE WORLD

The circumference of the earth is 25,000 miles. Imagine that you have a very long rope, which is tied around the middle of the earth at the equator, touching its surface. Then the rope is raised onto the ends of 1-foot-high poles all around its length. How much longer does the rope need to be so that it still reaches all the way around the circumference?

Solution on p. 200

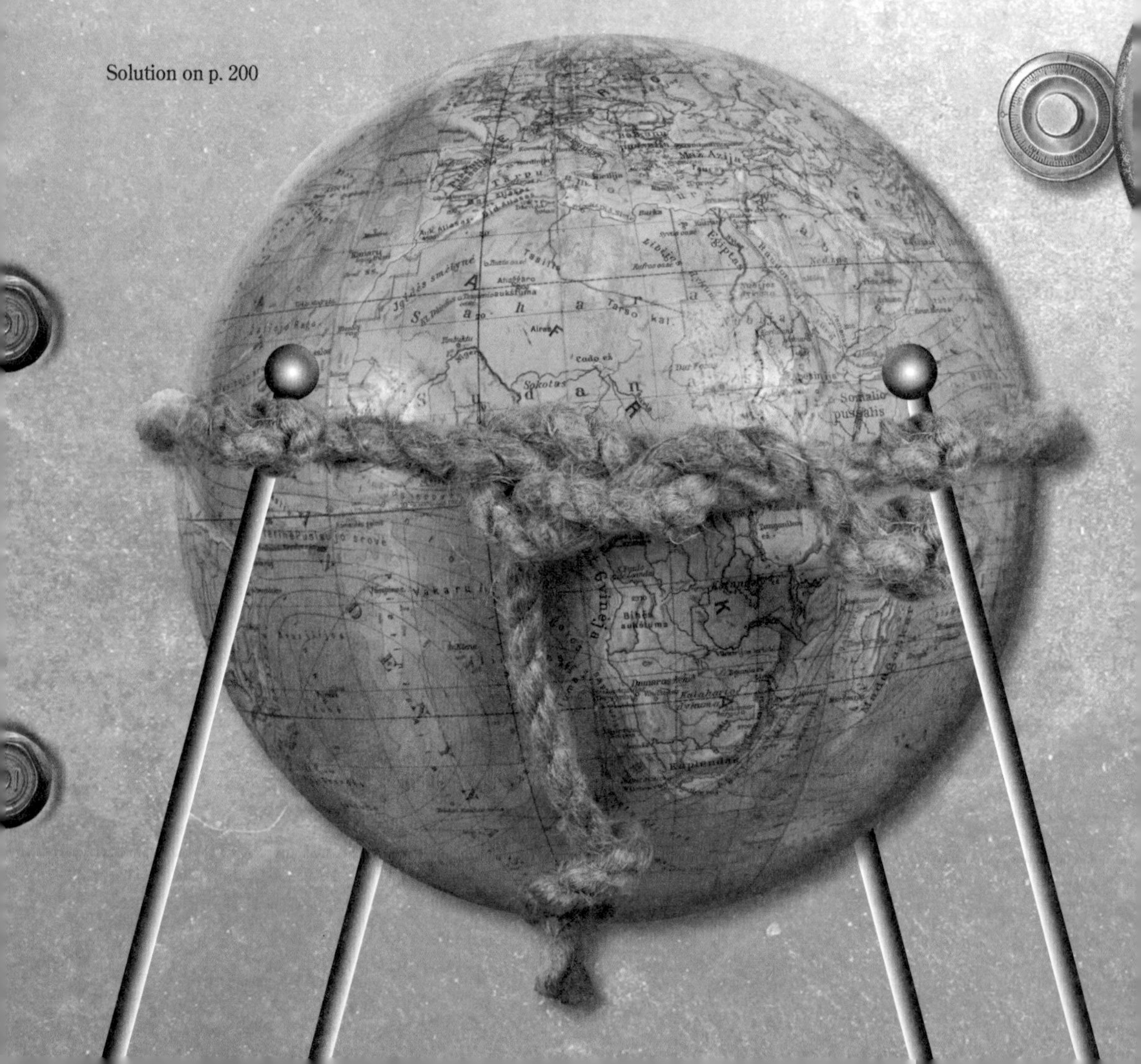

149 MATCH BRIDGE

Using just four matches, can you build a bridge between the two matchboxes?

Solution on p. 200

150 PAYDAY

Oliver and Arnold are walking home from the factory on payday, and each has the same amount of money as the other. How many dollars must Oliver give to Arnold so that Arnold has 10 dollars more than Oliver?

Solution on p. 201

151 MONEY

Replace the letters with numbers (0–9) to make this equation work (each letter represents a different number):

SEND + MORE = MONEY

Solution on p. 201

152 TEN PRISONERS

Ten dangerous prisoners are being held together in a large, round cell. The jailer needs to erect three circular electric fences inside the cell to separate all the prisoners from each other. Where should he put them?

Solution on p. 201

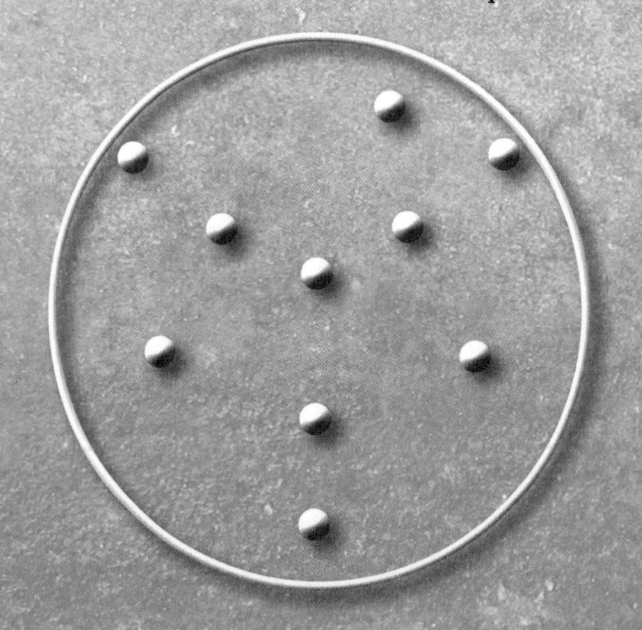

153 What Goes Around?

Which of the two small circles is perfectly round?

Solution on p. 201

154 FOUR FAUCETS

Boston's new municipal swimming pool has four faucets. On its own, the first faucet takes 12 hours to fill the pool, the second faucet takes 5 hours, the third faucet 10 hours and the fourth faucet takes 6 hours. How long does it take to fill the pool using all four faucets at once?

Solution on p. 201

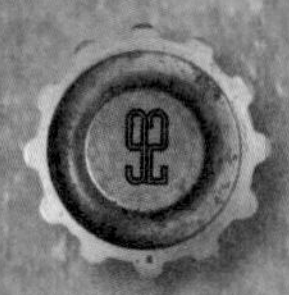

155 Something Fishy

Move three matches to make the fish below swim to the left.

Solution on p. 201

156 How Many Eggs?

Mrs. Thomas was not happy. Her daughter Caroline had returned from the farmers' market with a carton of very small eggs. "I only paid 12 cents for all of it," explained Caroline. "The farmer threw in two extra because they were small. So they cost 1 penny less per dozen than the price he had first offered."

How many eggs did Caroline buy?

Solution on p. 202

157 PUZZLING SCALES

Owen the palaeontologist is weighing his fossilized shell. How many marbles does the shell weigh if the top two scales are balanced? (There are 12 marbles in the top scale, 8 in the middle.)

Solution on p. 202

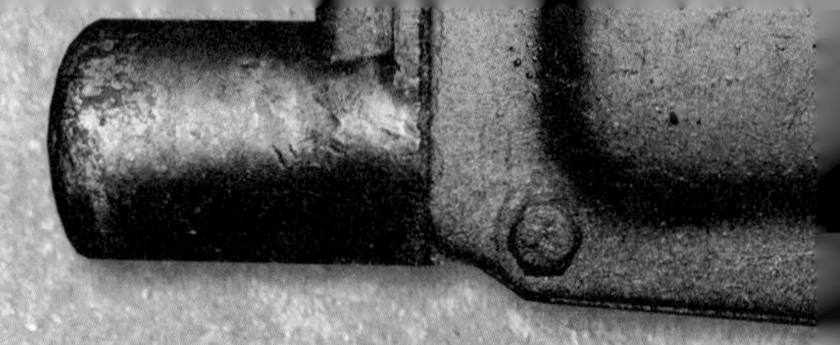

158 DRIVING TEST

Karl Benz wants to prove how good his new Motorwagen is by outrunning a horse-drawn carriage. He drives it at 16 mph, which is the car's top speed, and passes a carriage traveling at a constant 8 mph. How long must Benz keep on driving until he can stop for 15 minutes to let the engine cool down and start up again before he is overtaken by the carriage?

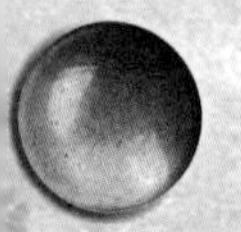

Solution on p. 202

159 A Happy Divorce

Barnabus and Florence are in love with each other.
They have been married for 20 years.
Barnabus tells Florence that he wants a divorce.
Florence is delighted.

Why?

Solution on p. 202

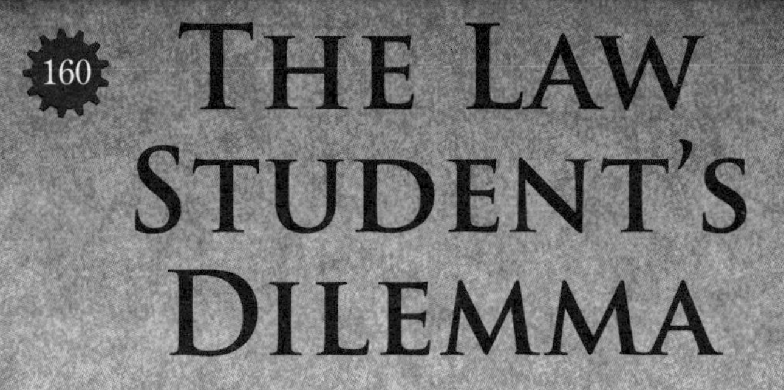

160 The Law Student's Dilemma

Here is a paradox from ancient Greece.

The teacher Protagoras agrees to take the penniless Euthalus as his student on the condition that Euthalus pays him for his tuition when he wins his first court case. Later, impatient for his money, Protagoras sues Euthalus for it, even though Euthalus has not yet won a case. Protagoras argues that if he wins the case, he will be owed the money, and that if Euthalus wins the case, he is still owed the money on the terms of the original contract. Euthalus, on the other hand, claims that if Protagoras wins the case, Euthalus still hasn't won a case, so he cannot be due to pay. If Euthalus wins the case, the terms of the original contract are voided, so he still does not have to pay.

Who is right, Protagoras or Euthalus?

Solution on p. 202

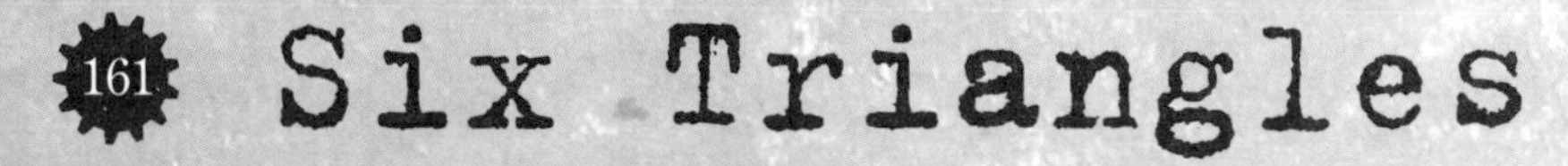

161 Six Triangles

Move two matches to leave six triangles.

Solution on p. 202

162 BLANK FACE

The ever-forgetful Professor Meade looked blankly for a second at the man standing in front of him. He reminded himself, "The son of this man is the father of my son."

Who was Professor Meade looking at?

Solution on p. 203

163

Buffon's Matches

French mathematician the Comte de Buffon figured out this puzzle. Draw a row of parallel lines on the floor that are two match-lengths apart. Now drop a whole box of matches, one by one, randomly on the area with the lines. After doing this, count the number of matches that lie across a line, and divide the total number of matches by this number.

What is the most likely result?

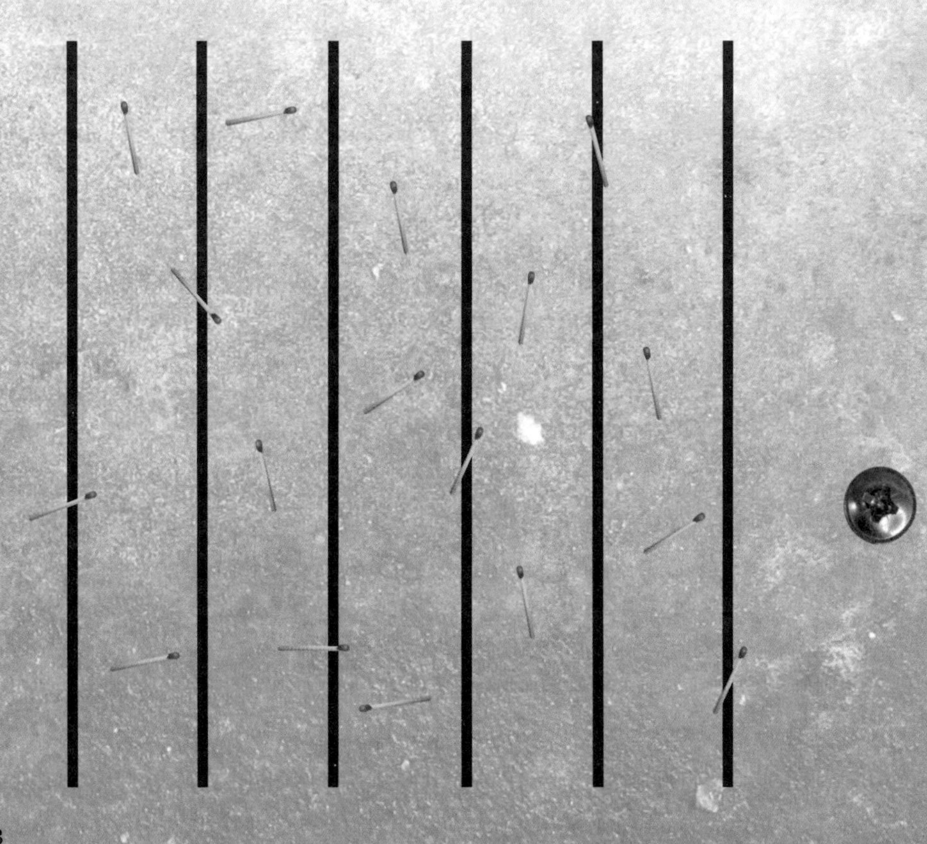

Solution on p. 203

164 How Old?

Andrea is half of her mother's age. Ten years ago, she was one-third of her mother's age.

How old is Andrea?

Solution on p. 203

165 Circular Sums

Substitute a number between 1 and 9 for each star so that the sum of the numbers in each circle is the same.

Solution on p. 203

166 A HAPPY OFFICE

Mr. Mainwaring is rearranging the clerks' desks at the bank. But he has a problem. Mr. Coltart wants to sit behind Miss Armitage, but Miss Armitage insists on sitting behind Mr. Coltart.

How does Mr. Mainwaring keep both his clerks happy?

Solution on p. 203

167 THE MISSING DOLLAR

Three weary travelers check into a hotel for the night. They are told that it will cost them $10 each, so they hand over $30 and get settled in. Later, the desk clerk realizes that he should only have charged them $25 because they had agreed to share the triple room. He gives the bellhop $5 to refund the travelers, but the bellhop is dishonest and pockets $2, refunding just $1 each to the travelers. So the travelers spent $27 and the bellhop kept $2. Where did the missing dollar go?

Solution on p. 203

168

A CABIN CONUNDRUM

In a small cabin in the woods, two men lie dead. The cabin itself is not burned, but the forest all around is burned to cinders.

How did the men die?

Solution on p. 203

169

THE TRUCK AND THE PIGEON

A full truck that weighs exactly 20 tons starts across a 10-mile bridge that can safely hold only vehicles that are exactly 20 tons or less in weight. Halfway across the bridge, a pigeon that weighs one pound lands on the truck. The bridge does not collapse.

Why not?

Solution on p. 204

170 Two Children

Walking along the street one day, Mr. Bartholomew remarked to a lady playing with two children of different ages, "What beautiful children you have." One of the children was a girl.

What are the chances that both children were girls?

Solution on p. 204

171 Three Squares

Move three matches to make three squares.

Solution on p. 204

172 Plane Crashes

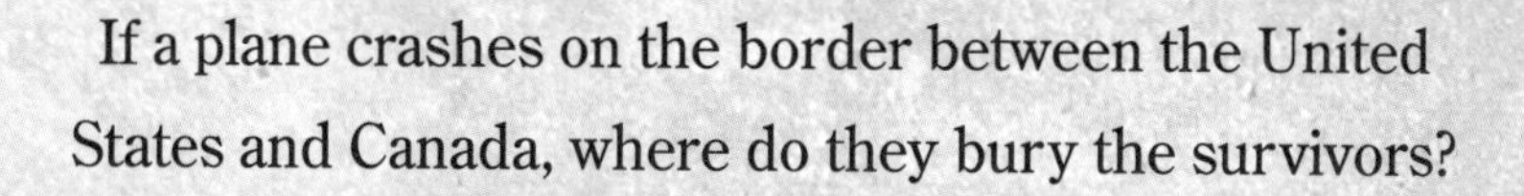

If a plane crashes on the border between the United States and Canada, where do they bury the survivors?

Solution on p. 204

173 SIX GLASSES

Mr. Overend has lined up six wine glasses in a row in front of him. The first three are filled with wine. The second three are empty. How can he make the row alternate between empty and full glasses by only moving one glass?

Solution on p. 204

174 Marbles

A condemned prisoner is given one last chance for a pardon by a king. The king hands him a bag of 50 black marbles, a bag of 50 white marbles, and two bowls. He is told that he must pour the marbles into the bowls. He may distribute the marbles between the two bowls as he wishes. He will then be blindfolded, the marbles will be swirled around in the bowls, and the bowls may also be switched around. He must then touch the outside of one of the bowls and take a marble from the bowl that he touched. If the marble is black, then he dies. If it is white, he is pardoned.

How should the prisoner distribute the marbles to give himself the best chance of survival?

Solution on p. 205

175 ALPHA BETA

Replace the letters with numbers (0–9) to make this equation work (each letter represents a different number):

ALFA + BETA + GAMA = DELTA

Solution on p. 205

176 Gone Fishing

Two fathers take their sons fishing. Each father and each son catches one fish, but when the men return home, they only have three fish between them. They did not throw any back, so how can that be?

Solution on p. 205

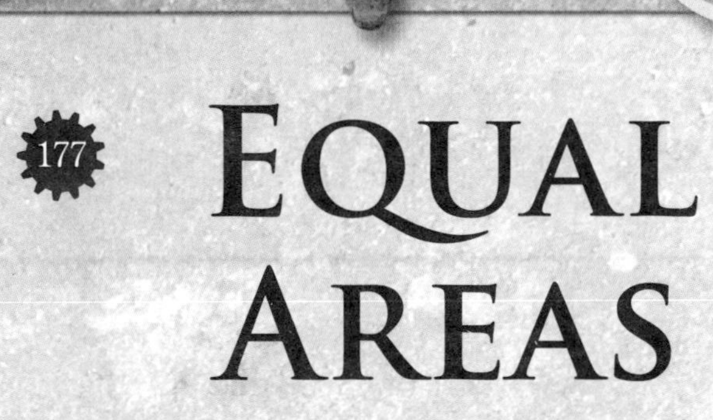

177 Equal Areas

Add four matches to divide the square into two parts of equal area and shape. You may not overlap or break the matches.

Solution on p. 205

178 Tunneling Test

A mile-long train traveling at 60 mph enters a mile-long tunnel. How long does it take for the entire train to pass through the tunnel?

Solution on p. 205

179 THE WASON TEST

These four cards are placed in front of you on a table. Each has a number on one side and a color on the other. Which cards should you turn over to prove the truth of the following statement: If a card shows an even number on one face, then its opposite face is red?

3 8

Solution on p. 205

180 Two Drunk Men

Two drunkards, Dum and Dee, stumble across a cask of wine with its lid removed on their way home. Peering into the cask, Dum the optimist thinks it is just over half full. Dee the pessimist thinks it is just over half empty. How can they find out who is right?

Solution on p. 206

181 PROBLEM PILLS

Dr. Fisher has a problem. He has 12 bottles of pills on the shelf marked "aspirin," but the labels on the bottles have been mixed up. One of Dr. Fisher's bottles of arsenic has disappeared, and he is worried that one of these 12 bottles contains deadly arsenic pills, instead of harmless aspirin. He does not know how many pills there are in each bottle, but he does know that one arsenic pill weighs 9 grams while an aspirin pill weighs 10 grams. Otherwise, they look identical. He has a very accurate scale but the batteries in it are almost dead, so he may only be able to use the scale once.

How can Dr. Fisher figure out which bottle, if any, contains the arsenic by making just one measurement with the scale?

Solution on p. 206

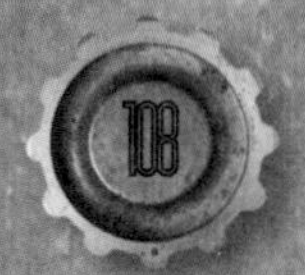

ROMEO'S LADDER

Romeo has a problem. He is anxious to climb the balcony to Juliet's bedroom, but he suffers from terrible vertigo, and now he is stuck on the middle rung of his ladder, afraid to go on. Thinking of his love, he steels himself and climbs four rungs, before falling back five rungs in a panic. He tries again, and this time manages six rungs, stops for a rest, then climbs the last six rungs and reaches the balcony.

How many rungs are there on Romeo's ladder?

Solution on p. 206

ABCDE

Replace the letters A, B, C, D, and E with the numbers 1, 2, 3, 4, and 5 so that the following equation works:

$$AB \times C = DE$$

Solution on p. 206

184 TRIANGLE AND A DIAMOND

Move two matches to make a triangle and a diamond.

Solution on p. 206

185 Popping Pills

Mrs. Fontague is feeling very sick. Her doctor prescribes her ten pills, one to be taken immediately, and the rest taken one at a time every 15 minutes after that. How long will it take Mrs. Fontague to finish her pills?

Solution on p. 206

186 Off to Market

As she strolled to market with nothing but an empty basket, Mrs. Tyler met seven farmers. Each farmer had three pigs. Three of the farmers had two sheep each, and one of the farmers had 15 geese.

How many feet were walking to market?

Solution on p. 206

187 Cue Power

A pool player wants to take his own cue to a tournament on an island resort, but his cue is nearly 5 feet long, and the ferry rules don't allow luggage more than 4 feet long. The player goes to see a carpenter, who makes him a new case for his cue out of very thin wood. The pool player is allowed on the ferry with his cue, carrying it in its new case.

What shape is the case?

Solution on p. 207

188 Four of a Kind

From a full deck of 52 cards, how many cards do you need to draw to guarantee you have four of a kind in your hand?

Solution on p. 207

189 Five Decks

Now, if you have five decks of cards, how many do you need to draw to guarantee four of a kind?

Solution on p. 207

190 Two Balls

Which of the orange circles is bigger?

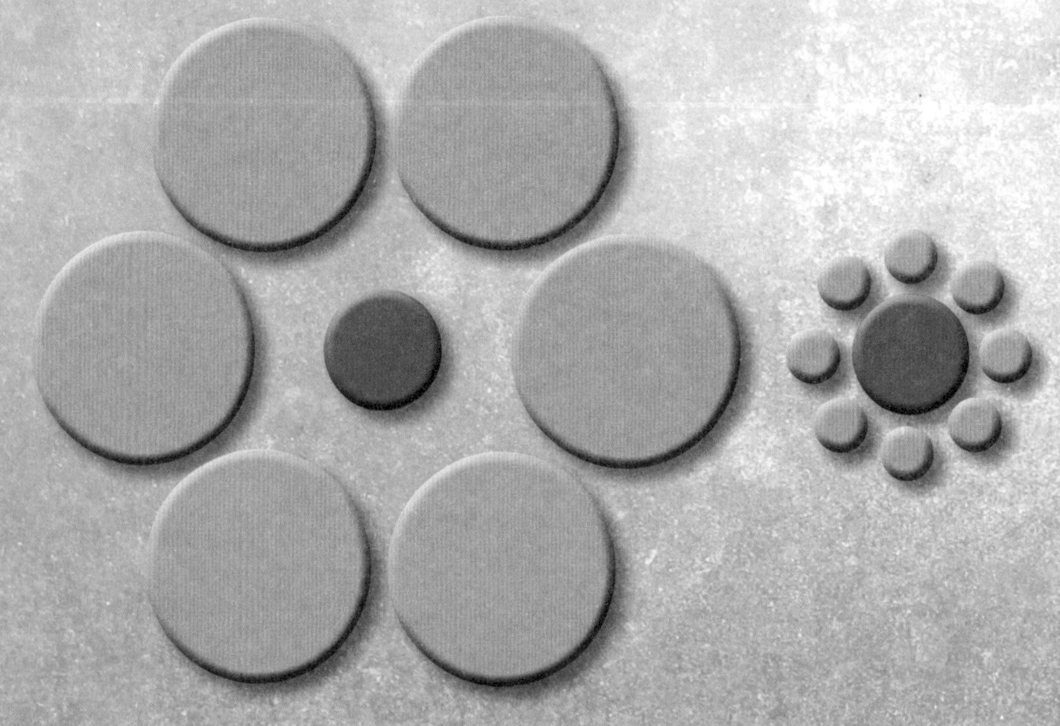

Solution on p. 207

191 MAKE A THIRD

Arrange the numbers 1, 2, 3, 4, 5, 6, 7, 8, and 9, using each just once, to create a fraction equal to ⅓.

Solution on p. 207

192 BREAK THE CHAIN

A jewelry maker wants to make one long silver chain out of four separate chains three links long. Every link she breaks she will have to solder back together again. How can she make her long chain with the minimum of soldering?

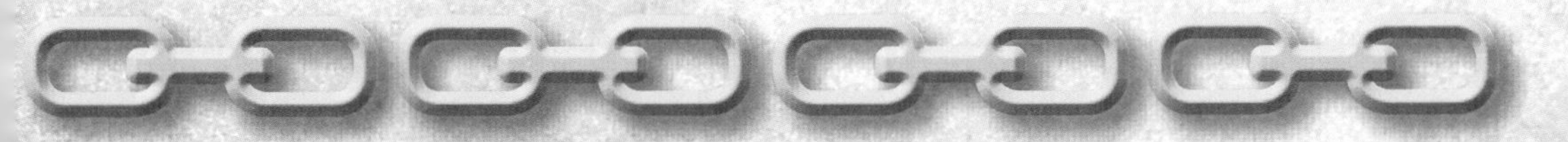

Solution on p. 207

193 ANGLES

What is the angle formed by the two dotted lines drawn on the sides of this cube?

Solution on p. 207

194 TEN BALLS

Place these ten balls in five lines so that each line has four balls on it.

Solution on p. 208

195 DIAMOND DILEMMA

Mr. Fulbright the gemologist has three diamonds and two boxes. One of the boxes is twice as long and twice as wide as the other. How can he put the diamonds in the boxes in such a way that each box contains an odd number of diamonds?

Solution on p. 208

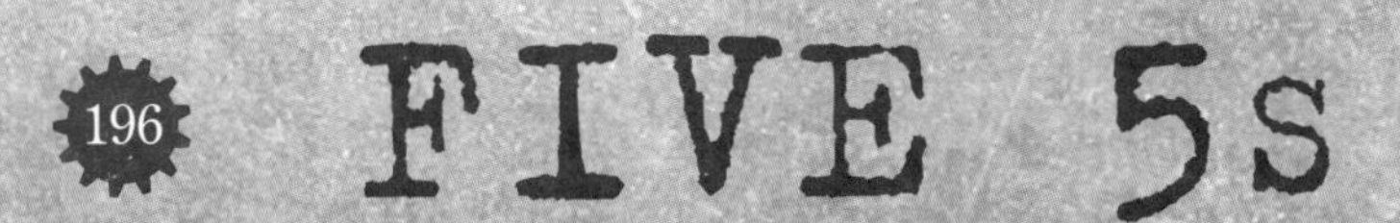

196 FIVE 5s

Replace the ?s with mathematical symbols to make this equation work (you can add parentheses, too):

5 ? 5 ? 5 ? 5 ? 5 = 100

Solution on p. 208

AGE CONCERN

Roger is ten times as old as his son, Matthew,
who is four times as old as his sister Theresa.
In 38 years' time, Roger will be twice as old as Theresa.

How old is Roger?

Solution on p. 208

WHAT TIME IS IT?

If it were two hours later, it would be half as long
until midnight as it would be if it were an hour later.

What time is it now?

Solution on p. 208

199 STRANGE EQUATION

How would you make this equation correct without changing it?

XI + I = X

Solution on p. 208

200 Slicing Problem

This large cube in made of 3 x 3 x 3 smaller cubes. How many times would you have to slice the large cube to completely separate all 27 of the smaller cubes?

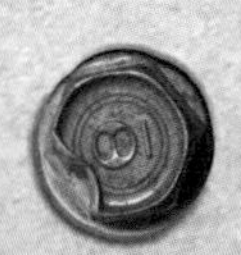

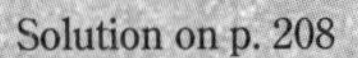

Solution on p. 208

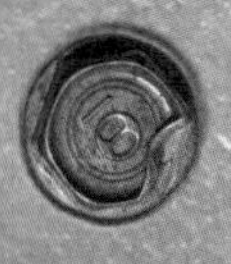

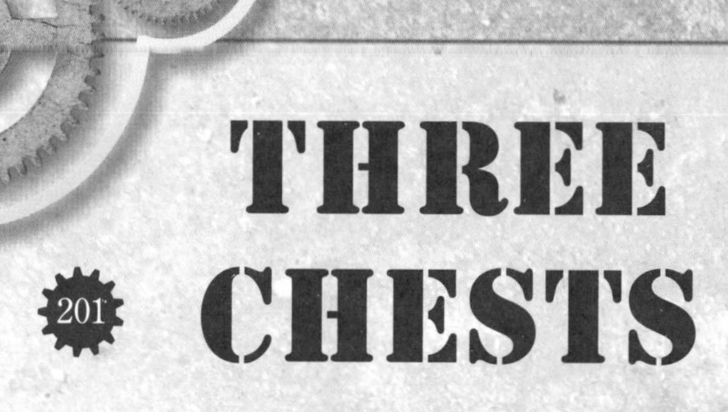

THREE CHESTS

201

Mr. Prowse presents his students with a puzzle each week. If they solve it, they can play a game of their choice. If they don't solve it, they have to do hard equations of his choice! This week, Mr. Prowse shows his class three chests.

"In one of the chests," says Mr. Prowse, "there are gold coins. In another chest are silver coins. And in the third chest there are bronze coins. The chests are labeled 'gold,' 'silver,' and 'gold or silver,' but all the labels are wrong. Now tell me, which chest contains which coins?"

Can you help Mr. Prowse's students?

Solution on p. 208

DIAMONDS

Move four matches to make five diamonds.

Solution on p. 209

Loose Change

Hermione has two coins left in her purse. Together they are worth 75 cents. The only coins that exist that are worth less than 75 cents are 1, 5, 10, 25, and 50-cent coins. If one of the coins is not a quarter, how much is each of Hermione's coins worth?

Solution on p. 209

204 Moving Pictures

Hold the book in your hands and focus your eyes on the black dot at the center of this figure. Now move the book toward you, then move it away from you again.

What can you see?

Solution on p. 209

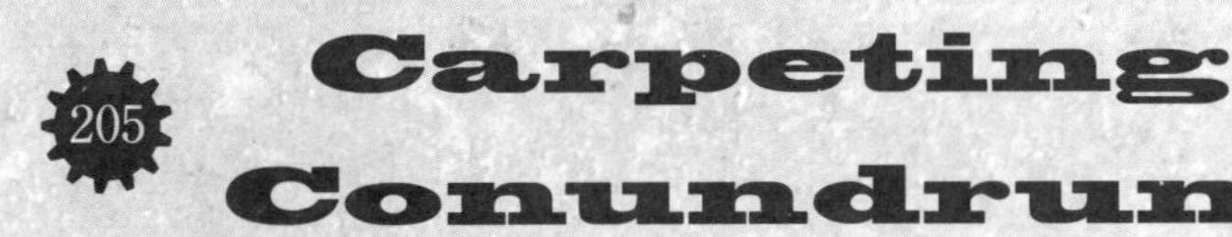

205 Carpeting Conundrum

Mrs. Williams is designing her dream house. One of the largest rooms in the house measures 9 yards by 12 yards. Mrs. Williams wants to split the space up by placing an aquarium measuring 8 yards by 1 yard in the center of the room, as shown here. She has a fine Egyptian carpet measuring 10 yards by 10 yards. How can she cut her carpet into two pieces of the same size that will fit the room perfectly?

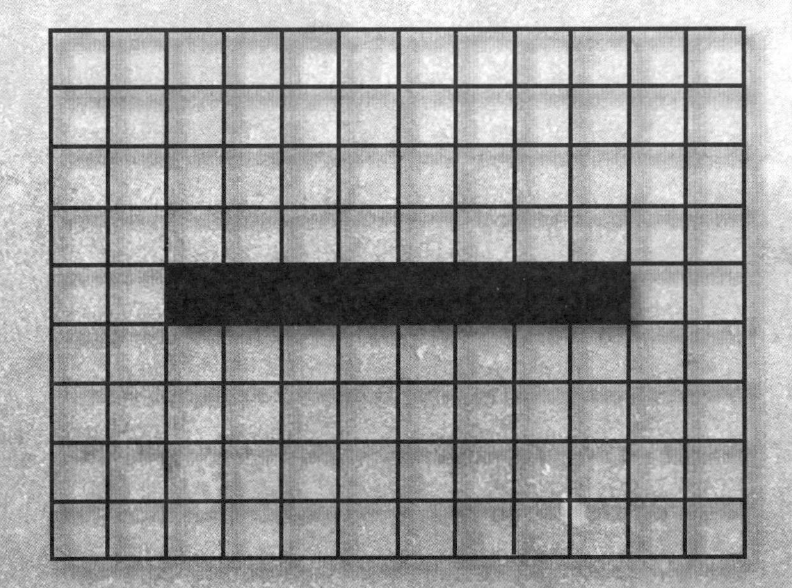

Solution on p. 209

206 Mental Arithmetic

Divide 30 by ½, then add 20 to the result.

What number do you get?

Solution on p. 209

207 Exam Room

Altogether, 360 schoolchildren sit down for their exams. Five percent of them have one pen. Of the remaining 95 percent, half of them have two pens, while the other half have none at all.

How many pens do the children have between them?

Solution on p. 209

208 SENSES

Helen is blind, deaf, and dumb.

How many of her five senses does she have left?

Solution on p. 209

Six Squares

Move eight matches to make six squares.

Solution on p. 210

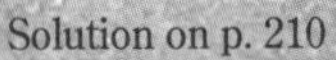

CAMPANOLOGY

The bell-ringer at St. Patrick's Cathedral takes 2 seconds to ring the bells at 3 o'clock. How long does it take her to ring the bells at noon?

Solution on p. 210

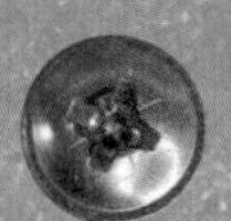

211 THREE SQUARES

Draw these three interlaced squares without lifting your pencil from the paper, without going over any line twice, and without crossing over any other line.

Solution on p. 210

212 SUBTRACTION

How many times can you subtract 6 from 36?

Solution on p. 210

213 HAPPY OR SAD

Which of these two fellows looks happier to you?

Solution on p. 211

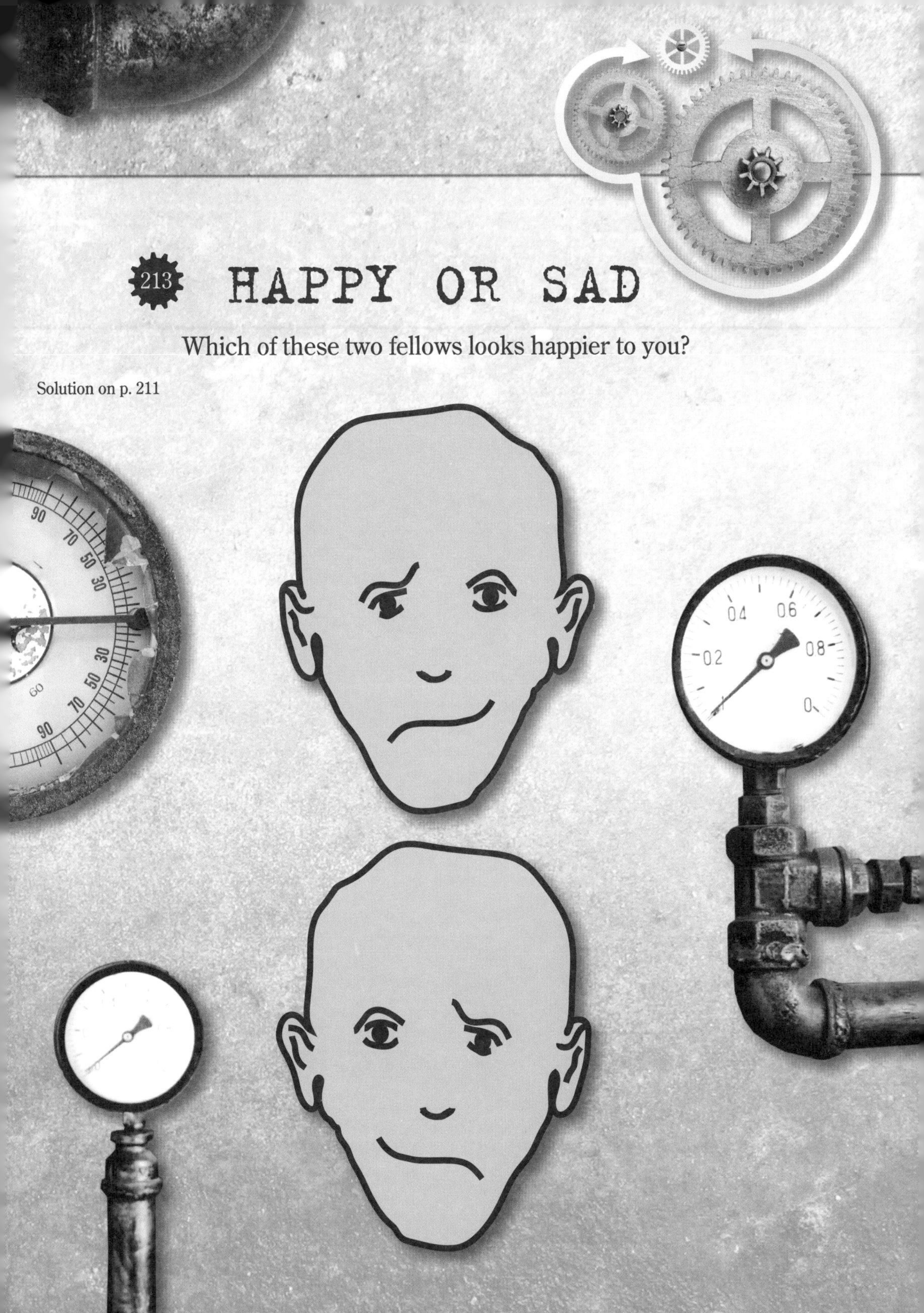

214 LAYING TIME

If 600 hens lay on average 600 eggs in eight days, how many eggs do 200 hens lay on average in two days?

Solution on p. 211

215 Touching Matches

Arrange these six matches so that each one touches the other five.

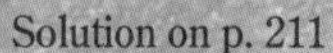

Solution on p. 211

216 EASY RIDER

A cowboy rides into Dodge City on Friday.
He stays for two nights, then rides out on Friday.

How?

Solution on p. 211

217 Cleaning Windows

William the window cleaner has fallen on hard times.
William laments: "The week before last week,
I earned less than 3 dollars. Last week, I earned only
a third of that, and this week, I earned less
than half as much as last week."
If he charges 25 cents per window cleaned and only
charges for whole windows, how much has William
earned in the last three weeks?

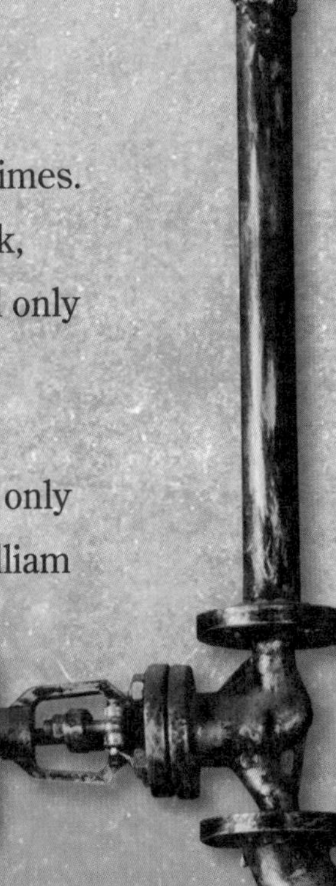

Solution on p. 211

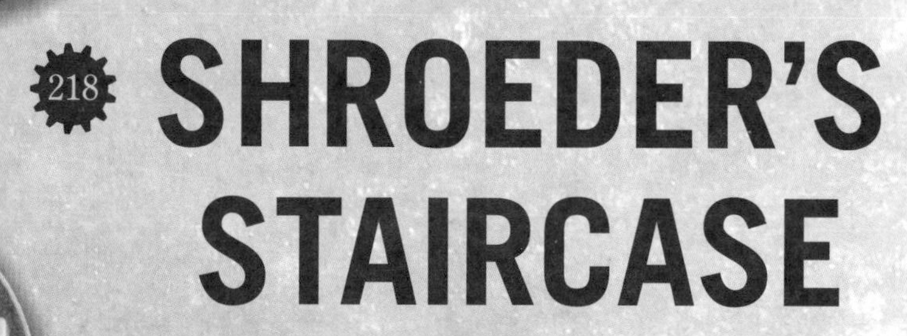

218 SHROEDER'S STAIRCASE

Which way do these stairs lead?

Solution on p. 211

219 STUCK

Replace the letters with numbers to make the following correct (each letter is a different number):

(S + T + U + C + K) x (S + T + U + C + K) x (S + T + U + C + K) = STUCK

Solution on p. 211

220 HENRY'S SPIRAL

The great Edwardian puzzler Henry Dudeney set this challenge. How did he draw this spiral using just a pencil, a compass, and the sheet of paper on which the diagram was made?

Solution on p. 212

221 CYCLES

A professional cyclist turns onto the highway, right past a sign saying “NO BICYCLES.” He passes a police car. The policeman sees him, but does nothing. Why didn’t the policeman pull the professional cyclist over?

Solution on p. 212

222 CORRECT THE EQUATION

Move two matches to make this equation correct.

Solution on p. 212

223 BAKING CAKES

A baker needs to bake three cakes, but he can fit only two cakes in the oven at a time. The cakes need to be baked for two minutes on each side. What is the minimum time the baker needs to bake all three cakes?

Solution on p. 212

224 Number Triangle

Place the numbers 1, 2, and 3 in the circles at each corner of the triangle. Now add the numbers 4–9 to the rest of the circles so that each side of the triangle adds up to 17.

Solution on p. 212

225 Find the Fake

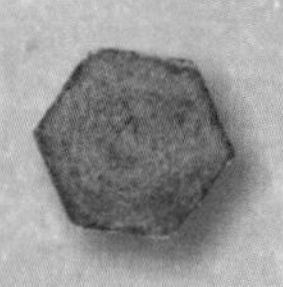

A man has brought 81 rubies to a gemologist for a valuation. The rubies are all the same size, but the man knows that one of them is a fake. He also knows that the fake weighs slightly more than the real jewels. Using this information, how can the gemologist identify the fake ruby using a scale by making just four weighings?

Solution on p. 213

226 ONE LINE

Draw this figure without lifting the pencil from the page, passing along the same route twice, or crossing over another line.

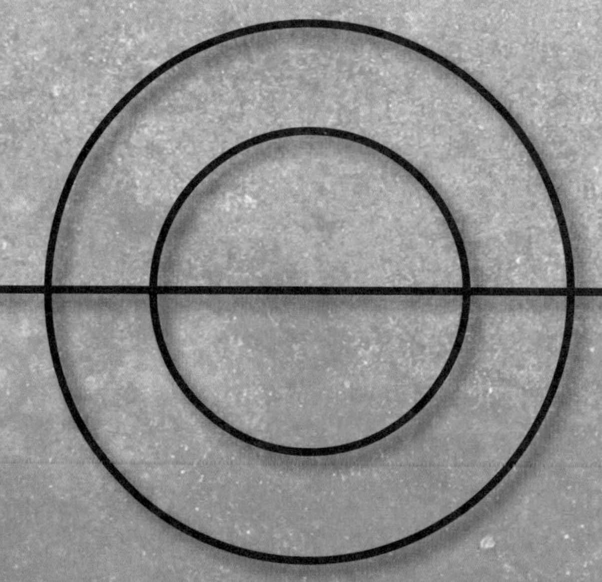

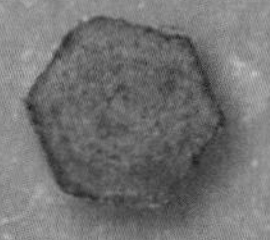

Solution on p. 213

227

MULTIPLICATION

Enter the numbers 0–9 in the following sum to make it work (3 has already been used and you can use each number only once):

3 x . . . . = ...

Solution on p. 213

228

SEVEN PILLARS

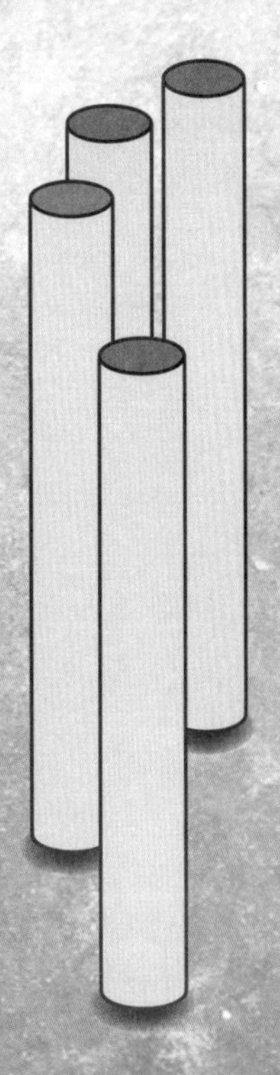

An architect has been commissioned to build Mr. Braxton a new country mansion. The huge house will have a grand ballroom with seven pillars in it. The architect wants to arrange the pillars in such a way that there will be five lines of three pillars.

How does he do this?

Solution on p. 214

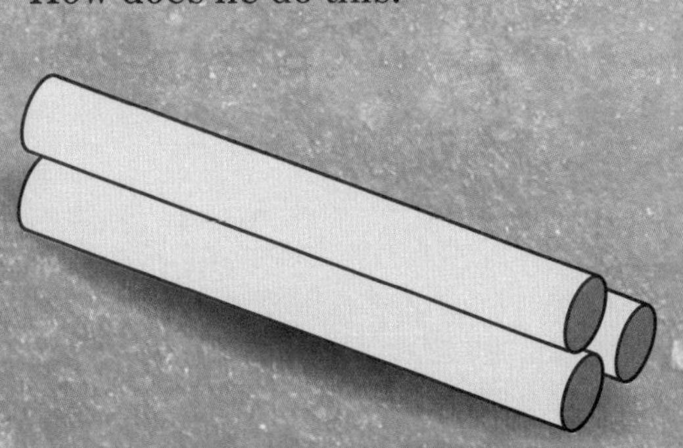

229 TURN OF THE CENTURY

In the year 1900, a woman makes the following calculation: she adds the year she was born to the year her daughter was born, then adds her current age and her daughter's current age.

What number does she come up with?

Solution on p. 214

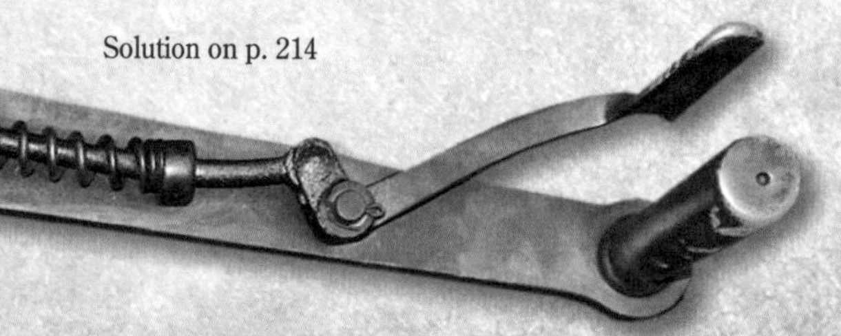

230 THREE COINS

A teacher places three coins in front of her pupil: one copper, one silver, and one gold. She tells her pupil, "If you tell me a true statement, you will be given one of the coins. But if your statement proves to be false, you will be given nothing."

What should the pupil say to guarantee being given the gold coin?

Solution on p. 214

231 MYSTERY MENU

Five men are staying in a hotel in a strange land where they do not know the language or customs. The hotel always offers the same nine dishes for dinner, listed as A, B, C, D, E, F, G, H, and I on the menu. The waiter won't tell them which dish is which letter, and when the dishes are brought out, they are set in the middle of the table in no particular order. If each man orders one dish each per night over three nights, how should they order if they want to figure out which dish is represented by each letter?

Solution on p. 214

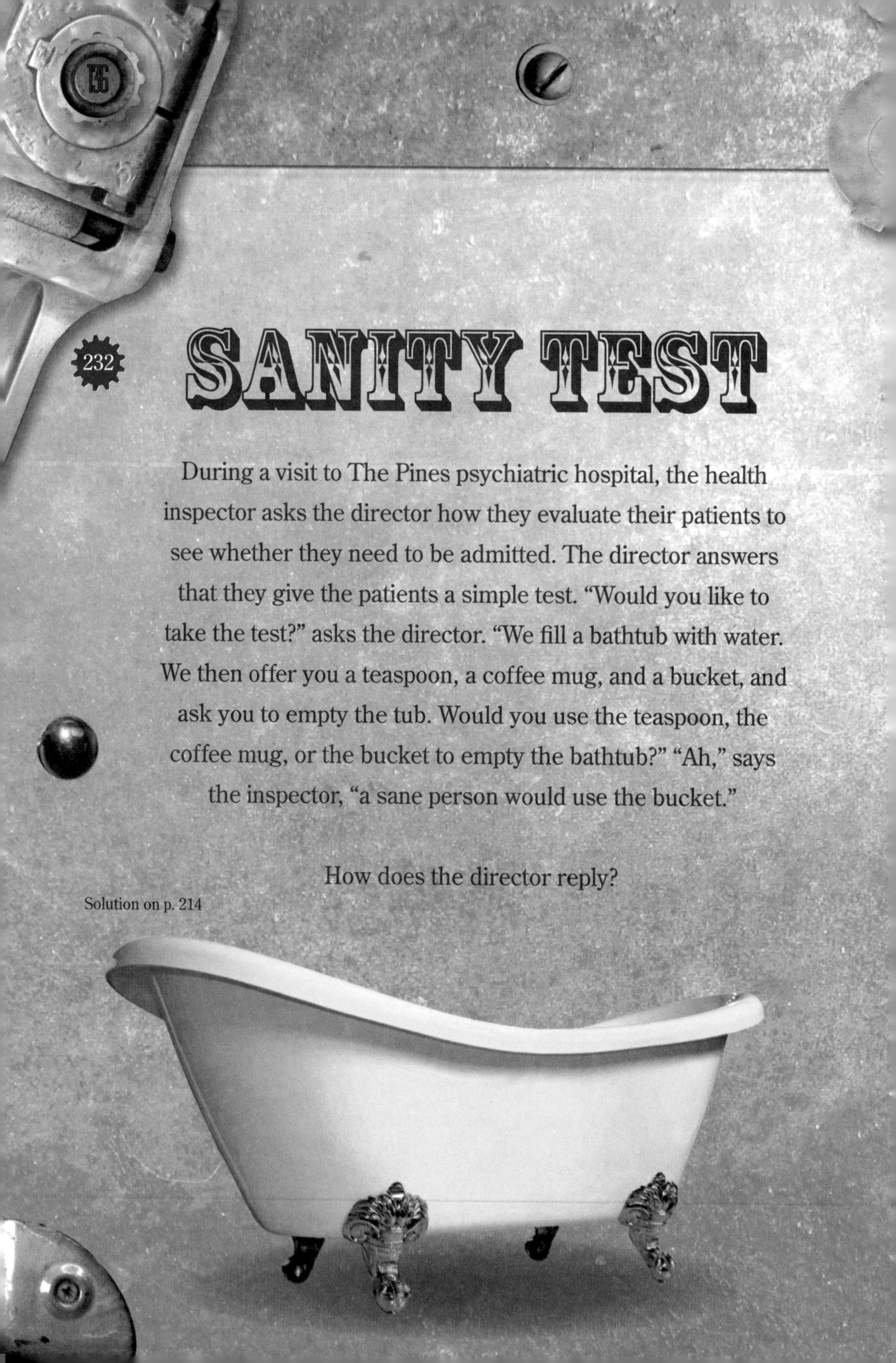

232

SANITY TEST

During a visit to The Pines psychiatric hospital, the health inspector asks the director how they evaluate their patients to see whether they need to be admitted. The director answers that they give the patients a simple test. "Would you like to take the test?" asks the director. "We fill a bathtub with water. We then offer you a teaspoon, a coffee mug, and a bucket, and ask you to empty the tub. Would you use the teaspoon, the coffee mug, or the bucket to empty the bathtub?" "Ah," says the inspector, "a sane person would use the bucket."

How does the director reply?

Solution on p. 214

233 Four Parts

Divide this shape into four identical parts.

Solution on p. 214

234 Siblings

Mr. and Mrs. Trevellian have four daughters.
Each of their daughters has one brother.

How many children do the Trevellians have?

Solution on p. 215

235 Five Squares

Remove four matches to leave five squares.

(There are two possible answers.)

Solution on p. 215

236 MOVE A FIGURE

Move one of the figures in the following equation to make it correct:

101 - 102 = 1

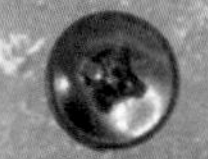

Solution on p. 215

237 BLIND MAN'S DECK

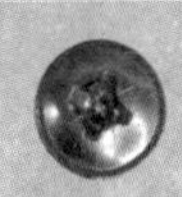

A blind man is handed a deck of 52 cards. He is told that ten of the cards are face up, the rest are face down. How can he divide the cards into two piles and make sure that each pile has the same number of cards facing up?

Solution on p. 215

238 I.T.

The computer and games console below both need to be connected to the hi-fi, the Internet, and the electrical outlet, as shown. Connect them in such a way that the cords do not touch or cross.

Solution on p. 215

239 Pen and Ink

A pen and ink pot together cost 22 dollars.
The pen is worth 20 dollars more than the ink pot.

How much does the pen on its own cost?

Solution on p. 215

240 Wheeler Dealer

A trader buys a roll of cloth for 60 dollars, then sells it for 70 dollars. Later in the day, he buys the same roll back for 80 dollars and sells it again for 90 dollars.

Was that a wise thing to do?

Solution on p. 215

241 A Gruesome Choice

A condemned man will be allowed
to choose the manner of his death.
He is given the following six options:

1 Thrown into a deep river, tied to a heavy stone.

2 Decapitated by an ax.

3 Eaten alive by a group of cannibals.

4 Thrown into a pit of lions that have not eaten for five months.

5 Hanged by the neck until he is dead.

6 Shot through the heart with a rifle.

Which option should he choose?

Solution on p. 216

242 How Many Holes?

If you fold a piece of paper in half, fold it in half again four more times, then cut off each of the four corners of the resulting rectangle, how many holes will there be when you unfold the paper again?

Solution on p. 216

243 A SQUARE

Make a square by moving one match.
(Think laterally!)

Solution on p. 216

244 Rummy

Emma and Jane are playing rummy during their lunch break. They agree to a small bet, and the winner of each round is given a jawbreaker by the loser. When the bell rings to return to class, Emma has won two games, but Jane has won three jawbreakers.

How many rounds of rummy did they play?

Solution on p. 216

245 EQUAL AREAS

Professor Snipe wants to divide her laboratory into four areas that are the same size and shape.

The plan is below. Can you help?

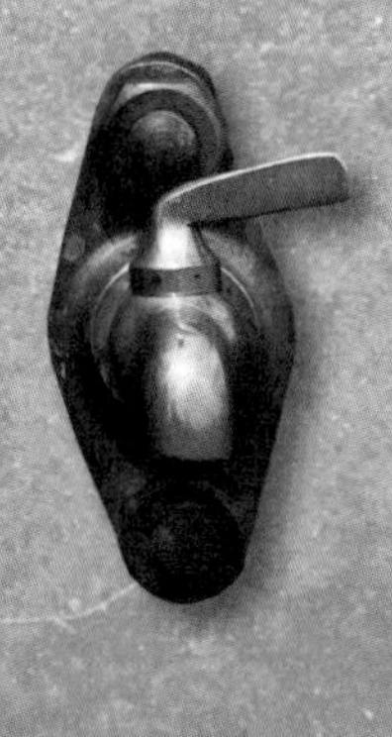

Solution on p. 216

246 Will and Testament

Mr. Samuels the billionaire has locked his last will and testament inside one of three boxes: a gold box, a sliver box, and a lead box. On each box is an inscription. At least one of the inscriptions is true and at least one of them is false.

The inscriptions are:

1. **Gold box**: The will is not in the silver box.
2. **Silver box**: The will is not in this box.
3. **Lead box**: The will is in this box.

His children can open just one box to read the will. If the box is empty, all of Mr. Samuels' fortune will go to charity.

Which box should they open?

Solution on p. 216

247

SUBTRACTION

Using the figures 7, 7, 7, 7, and 1, can you make the number 100 using just a minus sign?

Solution on p. 216

248

Late for Work

Arthur leaves for work one morning. Just as he's about to leave, he looks at the time in the mirror. The clock is an analog clock but doesn't have any numbers on it. Arthur forgets that it is a mirror image and reads the minute hand as the hour hand and the hour hand as the minute hand. He thinks he has plenty of time and strolls to work happily on a 20-minute walk. To his horror, when he gets to work, he finds out that the time is 2½ hours later than the time he saw on his clock.

What time did Arthur leave the house?

Solution on p. 216

249 HOW OLD?

A mother says to her son, "I am four times as old as you were when I was the same age as you are now."

If the mother is 40 years old, how old is her son?

Solution on p. 217

250 Moving Parts

A sundial is a timepiece with the fewest moving parts: It has no moving parts at all.

Which timepiece has the most moving parts?

Solution on p. 217

251 A NEVER-ENDING GAME

Fed up with the apathy of her class, a teacher devises a game to make them answer her questions. The class is split into three teams: the red, blue, and green teams. The teacher will ask questions and the pupils must put their hands up if they know the answer.

If the first pupil to answer correctly is from the red team, one of the blue team will be eliminated. If the correct pupil is from the blue team, one of the green team is eliminated. If they are from the green team, one of the red team is eliminated. The teacher will keep asking questions until only one team is left. Each member of that team will win a chocolate bar.

When she hears this, one clever pupil whispers to her classmates. The questions begin, and to her horror, the teacher finds that none of the pupils wants to answer correctly.

Why?

Solution on p. 217

252 Digital Clock

Move two matches to make the time half past four.

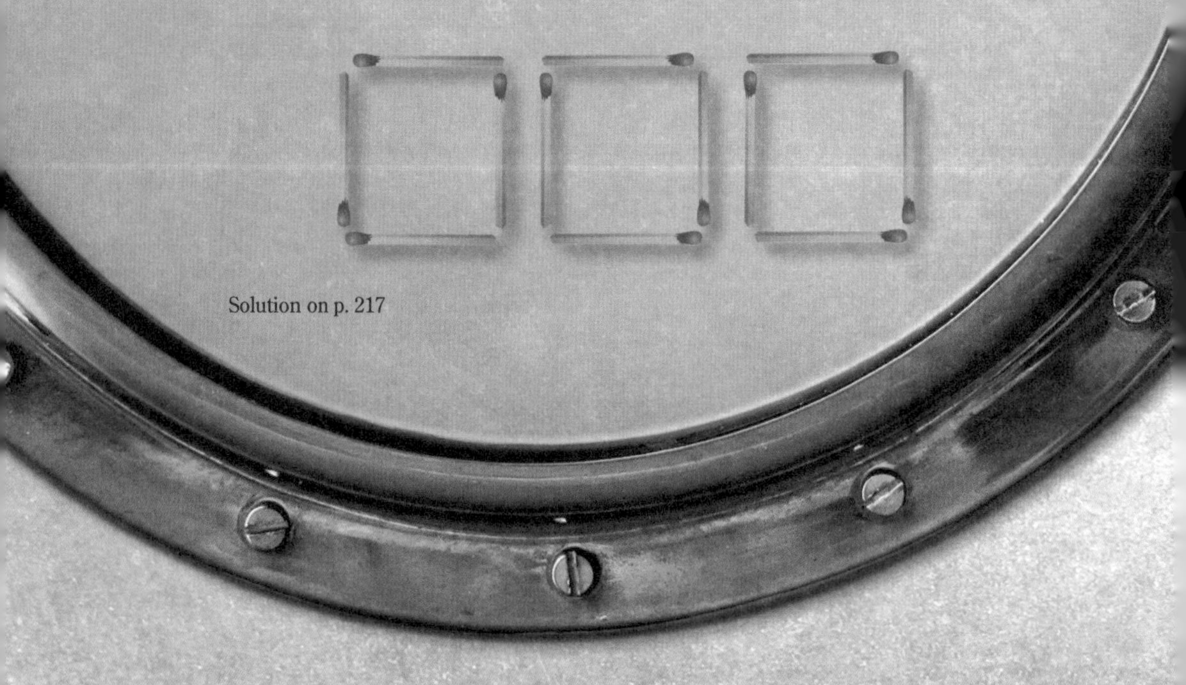

Solution on p. 217

253 

The hotel housekeeper keeps cats to make sure the kitchens are free of mice. Three cats can catch three mice in three minutes.

How many cats would the housekeeper need to catch 100 mice in 100 minutes?

Solution on p. 218

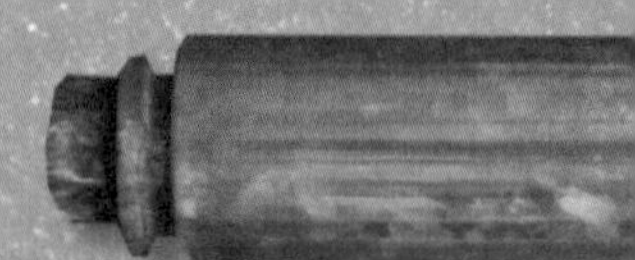

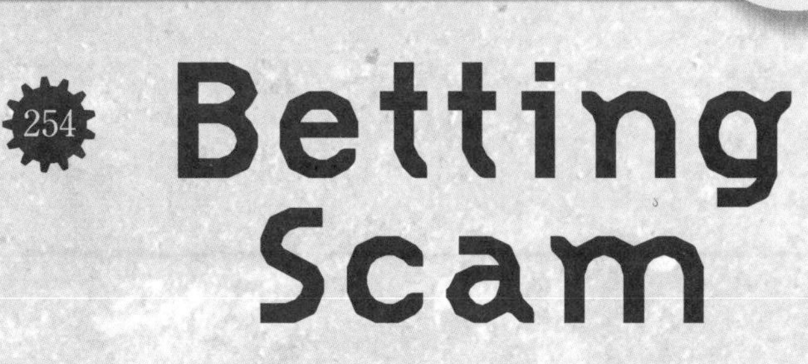

254 Betting Scam

One day, you receive an e-mail from a stranger telling you that he knows of a scam in which horse races are being fixed. To prove it, he predicts the result of a race that day. Sure enough, the 2–1 favorite wins as predicted. The next day, he e-mails you again saying that there's another fixed race. This time it's a 10–1 outsider, and again the prediction comes true. After a week, you have received six e-mails correctly predicting the results of six races. A seventh e-mail comes in. The stranger asks, "Would you like to place a $1,000 bet through me on the next fixed race? We can split the winnings."

Should you give him your money?

Solution on p. 218

255 WEIGH THE BABY

Standing on a scale holding her baby and her cat, a woman weighs 170 pounds. If the woman weighs 100 pounds more than the combined weight of her baby and her cat, and the cat weighs 60 percent less than the baby, how much does the baby weigh?

Solution on p. 218

256 Numbers for Letters

Replace the letters with numbers to make this work:

ABCD x E = DCBA

Solution on p. 218

257 FAMILY TIES

Annabel has three sisters. All four women are mothers. Her sister Beatrice has two nephews and three nieces. Her sister Carla has one nephew and three nieces. Her sister Davina has one nephew and five nieces. Annabel herself has one daughter and no sons.

How many nephews and nieces does Annabel have?

Solution on p. 218

258 SIX STRAIGHT LINES

How would you draw six straight lines to link these 16 points without lifting the pen from the paper?

Solution on p. 218

THINK LATERALLY!

Move one match to make this equation correct.

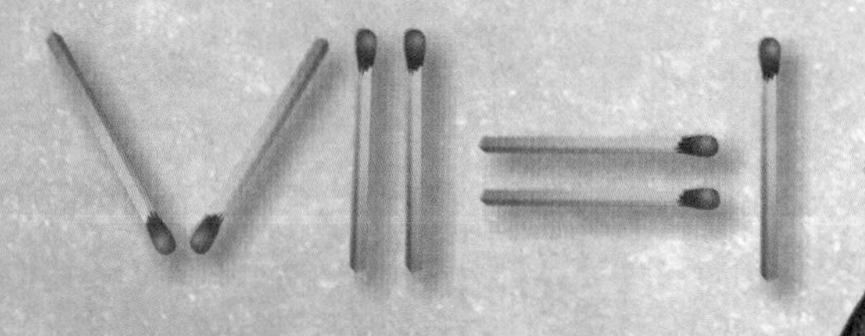

Solution on p. 218

A FAIR WEIGHT

A man and his son are carrying a pig to the market with its feet all tied together at one point on a pole. The man puts the front of the pole on his shoulder, while and his son takes the back. The distance from shoulder to shoulder is 5 feet.

Where should the pig's feet be tied on the pole if it weighs 100 pounds, the stronger man should be bearing 60 pounds and his boy 40 pounds?

Solution on p. 219

CLAIRVOYANT

A mystic has been summoned to a haunted house to discover a spirit dwelling there. She can sense that it must be present behind one of four doors, but each door is inscribed with a riddle written by the spirit:

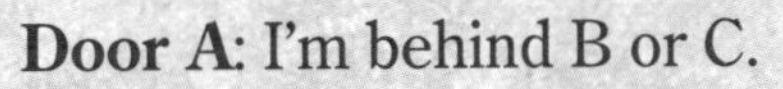

Door A: I'm behind B or C.

Door B: I'm behind A or D.

Door C: I'm in here.

Door D: I'm not in here.

The mystic knows that just one of these inscriptions tells the truth.

Where is the spirit?

Solution on p. 219

Make 24

Using the numbers 5, 5, 5, and 1 once each, make an equation whose result equals 24. You can use the mathematical operations of addition, multiplication, subtraction, or division.

Solution on p. 219

263 Car Crash

A man and his son are involved in a terrible car accident. The man dies instantly. The son is very badly injured and is taken to the hospital by an ambulance. He is rushed to the operating room, where the doctor exclaims, "Oh no, this is my son!"

How can this be?

Solution on p. 219

264 Arrange the Numbers

Place the numbers 1–8 in the squares so that no number is in contact on any side or diagonal with any number that is one greater or one less than it. So, for instance, 4 cannot not be next to 3 or 5.

Solution on p. 219

265 BEAR HUNTING

A hunter spots a bear very close to him, but the bear does not see him, so the hunter decides to sneak up on it. He walks 5 miles due south, then turns to walk 5 miles east before turning again to walk 5 miles north. To his horror, at the end of his hike, he finds himself face to face with the bear, which has not moved an inch.

The question is this: What color is the bear?

Solution on p. 219

266 Next Number

What is the next number in the following sequence?

8,643, 3,864, 4,386, ??

Solution on p. 219

267 DOTTY

Divide this triangle into four exactly equal areas, each containing the same number of dots.

Solution on p. 219

268 Weather Forecast

Cynical Cyril is watching television. At the end of the late-night movie, the weather forecast comes on. The weatherman says, “It is raining now and will continue to rain for another two days. However, in 72 hours' time, it will be bright and sunny!”

“Wrong again,” snorts Cyril.

How does he know that the forecast is wrong?

Solution on p. 220

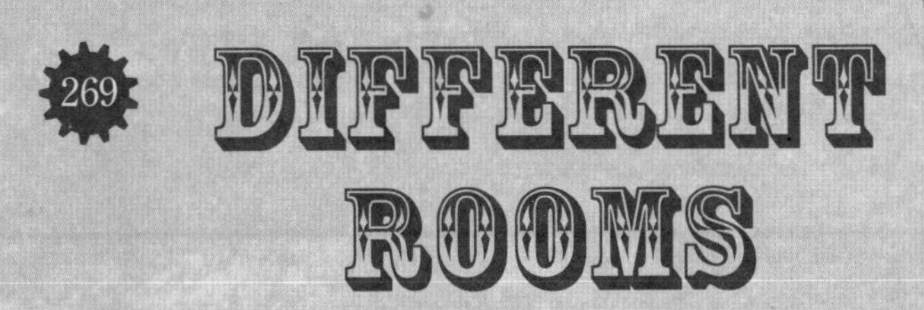

269 DIFFERENT ROOMS

Sylvester walks into a room. He turns around, stands there for a while thinking about this and that, then walks out of the room using the same door he came in through, but this time walking into a different room from the one he had started off in.

How?

Solution on p. 220

270 Three Triangles

Move four matches to make one large triangle and two small ones.

Solution on p. 220

271 ANNIVERSARY BLUES

A restaurant runs a deal in which couples are given a free bottle of champagne if it is their wedding anniversary, but they have to bring their certificate to prove it. One Thursday evening, a couple turns up without their certificate and claims their free drinks. The manager is called, and he asks what year they are celebrating. The woman replies that it is their 28th anniversary. The manager asks her to describe her wedding day to him. She effuses, "It was a wonderful, clear Sunday afternoon—unseasonably warm so we held the reception in the yard ..."

The manager waits to hear the end of the woman's story, then throws the couple out.

How did he know that she was lying?

Solution on p. 220

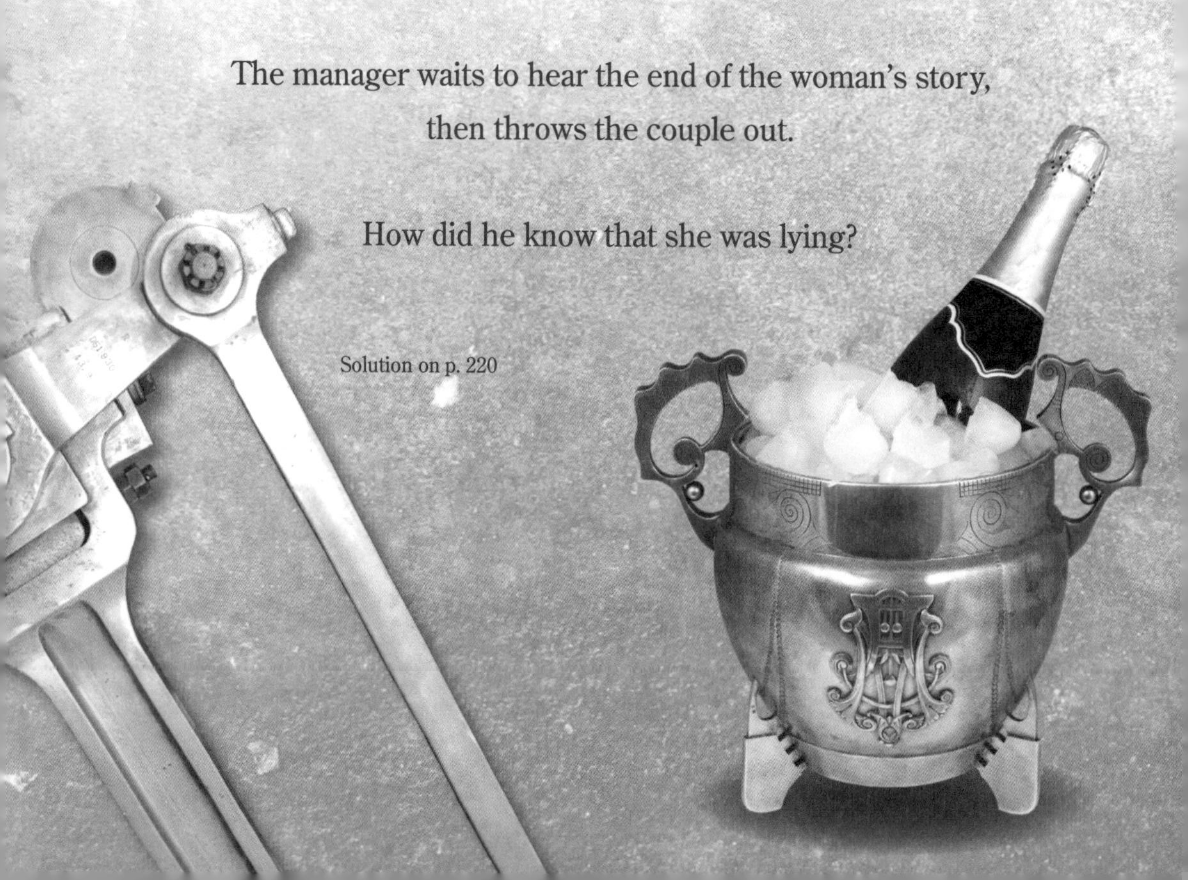

272 Next Number

What is the next number in this sequence?

0, 1, 1, 2, 4, 7, 13, 24, 44, ?

Solution on p. 220

273 SCHOOL PARTY

Three mothers, June, Claire, and Jennifer, are at the annual school party, where the parents are supposed to bring their own food. June has brought along five dishes and Claire has brought three. An embarrassed Jennifer has nothing. To save Jennifer's blushes, the other two women agree that they should share the dishes equally among them.

Jennifer has $8 dollars on her and offers to pay for what she has eaten by sharing the money between the other two. She suggests paying June $5 and Claire $3.

This is not a fair deal. Why not?

Solution on p. 220

274 SIX SQUARES

Move three matches to make a figure that contains six squares of the same size.

Solution on p. 220

275 HORSE RACE

Two cowboys have applied for the same job. The ranch manager tells them to ride up to the top of the nearby hill. The one whose horse reaches the summit second will get the job.

The two men jump on a horse and race each other at full gallop to the top of the hill. They both want the job, so why did they do that?

Solution on p. 220

276 HIGH DRAMA

The tightrope walker at Bartram's Circus uses a pole that is 3 feet long to help him to balance. He usually holds the pole with his hands about 2 feet apart, his palms pointing upward.

One night, when halfway along the tightrope, he has a major wobble and the pole slides through his hands so that one end of the pole is now very close to his left hand. Recovering his balance and taking a deep breath, he very carefully slides his hands toward each other at the same speed.

Which way does the pole fall?

Solution on p. 220

277 FOUR SQUARES

Make four identical squares that all touch each other by moving three matches.

Solution on p. 221

278 Missing Number

What is the missing number in this series?

???, 130, -1,690, 21,970, -285,610

Solution on p. 221

Birthday Party

At a child's birthday party, there are four mothers with their children, 1, 2, 3, and 4 years of age.

It is Juliet's child's birthday party.
Dylan is not the oldest child.
Anne had Holly just over a year ago.
Laura's child will be 3 on his next birthday.
Graham is older than Jamie.
Monica's child is the oldest.
Jamie is older than Laura's child.

Whose child is whose, and how old is each child?

Solution on p. 221

280 CONNECT THE DOTS

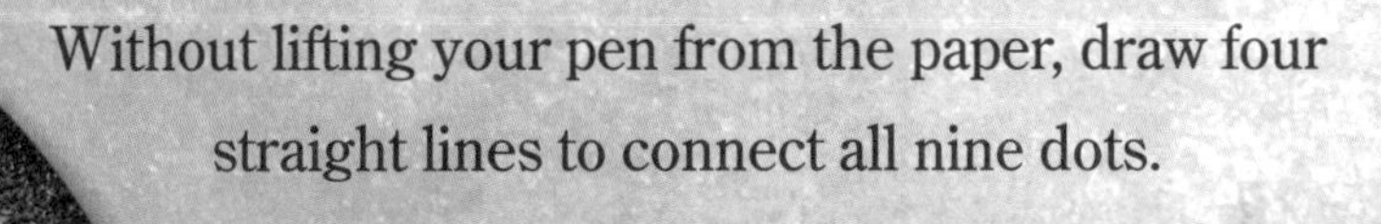

Without lifting your pen from the paper, draw four straight lines to connect all nine dots.

Solution on p. 221

281 Pirates

Captain Blighty's ship is captured by pirates. Before stealing the ship's cargo, the pirates decapitate Captain Blighty and hang his first mate. The rest of the officers lose their head.

The pirates only killed two men. How is this possible?

Solution on p. 221

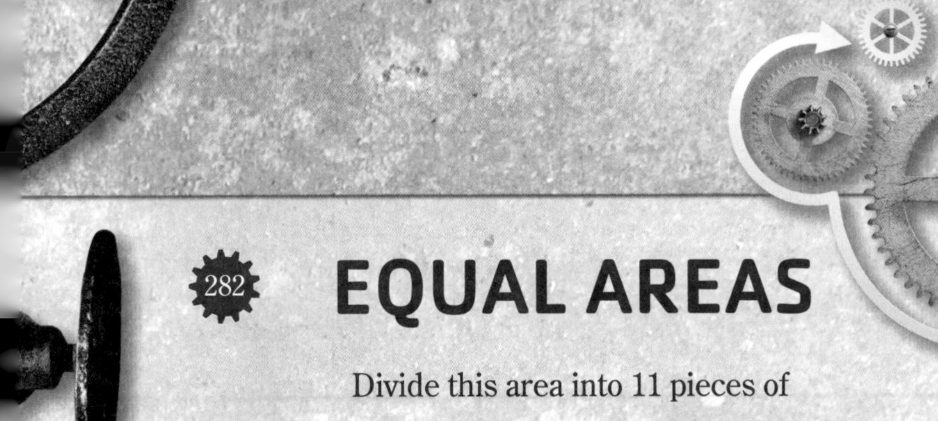

282

EQUAL AREAS

Divide this area into 11 pieces of equal size using 30 matches.

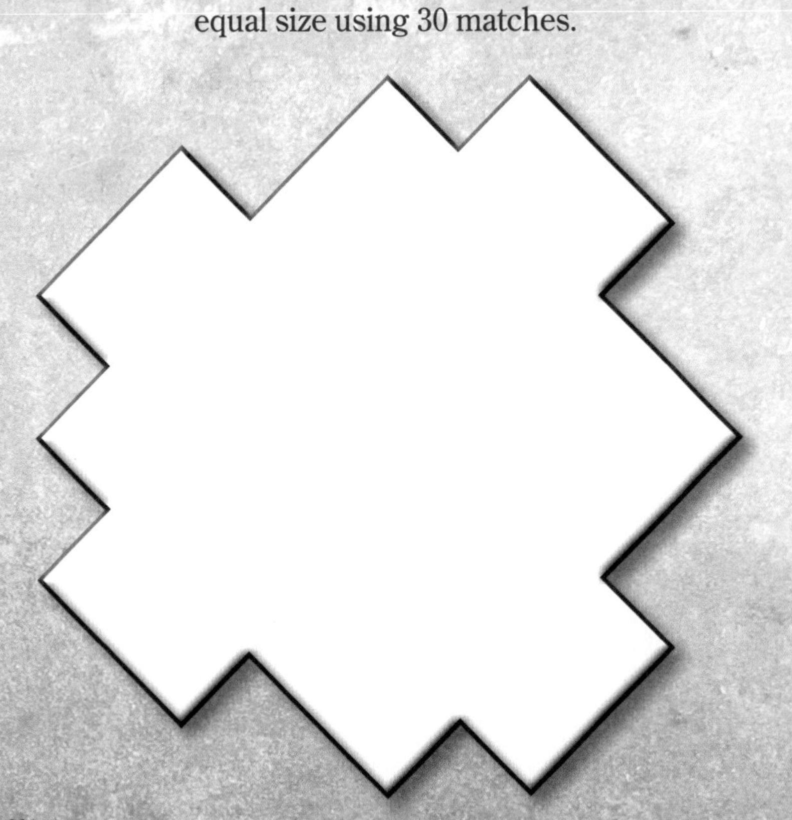

Solution on p. 221

283

COLOR MAP

What is the fewest number of colors you need to color in a map of the United States in such a way that no state is touching another state of the same color?

Solution on p. 221

284 THREE SUSPECTS

Three pickpockets are brought into Detective Vegas's office and made to stand in a line for questioning. Bruce is standing between the clean-shaven man and the man who stole the purse. Crusoe, who stole the wallet, was arrested at the same time as Watson. It was the man with the moustache, not the man with the beard, who stole the watch.

Which man stole which item, and who has what facial hair?

Solution on p. 221

285 HALVING THE SQUARE

Waylon took the wrong measurements. To make his painting, he needs a square piece of paper 50 square inches in size, but he has one that is 100 square inches. Given that he only wants to paint on one side of the paper, how can Waylon make it the right size when he doesn't have a ruler or scissors?

Solution on p. 222

286 Game of Chance

A casino runs a game of chance involving bets on the throw of three dice. For a $1 stake, a gambler gets to choose a number from 1 to 6. The dice are then thrown. If their number does not come up on any of the dice, they lose the bet. If their number comes up once, they win $2 (including the stake). If it comes up twice, they win $4, and if it comes up all three times, they win $6.

In the long run, does the house win in this game, or do the gamblers win?

Solution on p. 222

287 CROSS INTO A SQUARE

By making just two cuts with a pair of scissors, how would you turn this cross into a square?

Solution on p. 222

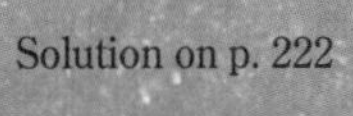

288 EQUAL AREAS

Using eight matches, divide this shape into four areas the same size and shape.

Solution on p. 222

Replace the Letters

Replace the following letters with numbers to make the equation work (each letter represents a different number):

ABCD x D = DCBA

Solution on p. 223

290 PHANTOM DOTS

Can you see the gray dots in this figure? Are they ever in the center of your visual field?

Solution on p. 223

291 A CLOSE SHAVE?

As he has grown older, James has become very farsighted. He can no longer focus on anything that is less than 2 feet away. He still enjoys a wet shave every morning, however. How far away from the mirror does James have to be to focus on his face as he shaves?

Solution on p. 223

292 NINE DIAMONDS

Remove four matches to leave nine diamonds.

Solution on p. 223

293 MISSING NUMBER

What is the missing number in this series?

46, 10, 82
29, 11, 47
96, 15, 78
54, 9, 72
42, ??, 15

Solution on p. 223

294 SLIPPING LADDER

Carl the roofer has just had quite a scare. He was clearing a gutter at the top of a 25-foot ladder. The foot of the ladder was 7 feet away from the wall at what Carl thought was a safe angle, but the ladder has just slipped, and the top of the ladder where Carl was working has gone down by 4 feet.

How far has the foot of the ladder moved?

Solution on p. 223

295 What Time Is It?

Time is really dragging at work for Marjorie. At noon, she looks over at the clock on the wall. The big hand is on the seven, while the little hand is between the four and the five.

What time is it?

Solution on p. 224

296 Seven Diamonds

Move four matches to make seven diamonds.

Solution on p. 224

297 Peeling Potatoes

Helen has a pile of 55 potatoes in front of her. She begins peeling them at a rate of two potatoes per minute. Five minutes later, seeing how slow Helen is working, her mother Grace joins in, peeling at a rate of five potatoes per minute. How long does it take them to peel the potatoes, and how many were peeled by each woman? (Once one of them has started on a potato, she has to finish it herself.)

Solution on p. 224

298 What Year?

The year 1978 has a special property.
If you add 19 to 78, the result of the sum is
equal to the year's middle two digits, 97.

What will be the next year with this property?
And the year after that one?

Solution on p. 224

299 CORK IN A GLASS

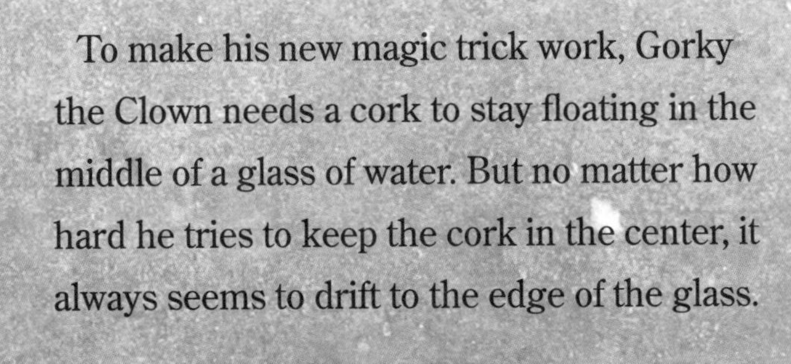

To make his new magic trick work, Gorky the Clown needs a cork to stay floating in the middle of a glass of water. But no matter how hard he tries to keep the cork in the center, it always seems to drift to the edge of the glass.

How would you help Gorky with his new trick?

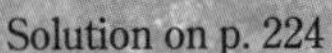

Solution on p. 224

300 Einstein's Riddle

And finally, here's a fiendish teaser from Albert Einstein, written at a time when a lot of people smoked!

In a certain street, there are five houses painted five different colors. In each house lives a person of a different nationality. Each person drinks a different kind of beverage, smokes a different brand of cigar, and keeps a different kind of pet. We know these 15 facts:

1. The Brit lives in the red house.

2. The Swede keeps dogs as pets.

3. The Dane drinks tea.

4. The green house is on the immediate left of the white house.

5. The green house's owner drinks coffee.

6. The owner who smokes Pall Mall rears birds.

7. The owner of the yellow house smokes Dunhill.

8. The owner living in the middle house drinks milk.

9. The Norwegian lives in the first house.

10. The owner who smokes Blends lives next to the one who keeps cats.

11. The owner who keeps the horse lives next to the one who smokes Dunhill.

12. The owner who smokes Bluemasters drinks beer.

13. The German smokes Prince.

14. The Norwegian lives next to the blue house.

15. The owner who smokes Blends lives next to the one who drinks water.

The question is: Who owns the fish?

Solution on p. 224

ANSWERS

1 He was 12 years old. Feb. 29, 1896, was a Saturday; Feb. 29, 1904, was a Monday. Remember that the year 1900 was NOT a leap year.

2

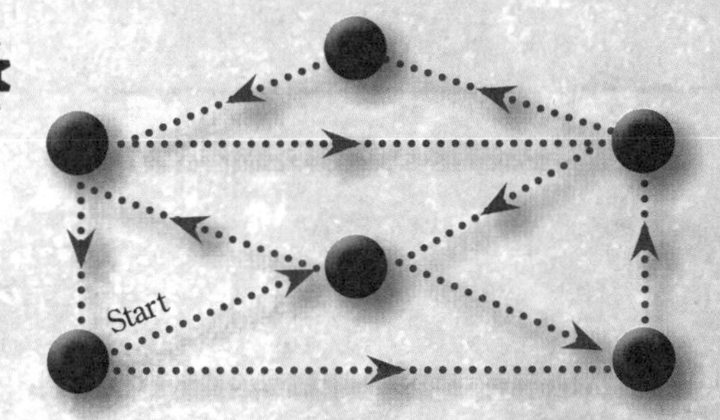

3 First Connie puts the message in the box and locks it with her padlock. She then sends the box to Daniel. Daniel attaches his padlock to the box and sends it back to Connie with both locks in place. Now, Connie removes her lock and sends the box once again to Daniel, this time with just Daniel's padlock on it. Daniel can now open the box and read Connie's secret message.

4 He traveled 110 miles. The next palindrome is 16,061 miles.

5

6 It is Tuesday.

29. The pattern being followed is: $a+b=c$, $b+c=d$, $c+d=e$, etc.

9

Adam is standing inside his cube.

Do you see the circle?

Five rungs are showing. The boat rises with the water level, so the number of rungs showing is unchanged.

He was 84.

If you call his total life x, you can make the following equation:

$\frac{1}{6}x + \frac{1}{12}x + \frac{1}{7}x + 5 + \frac{1}{2}x + 4 = x$

The solution to the equation is 84.

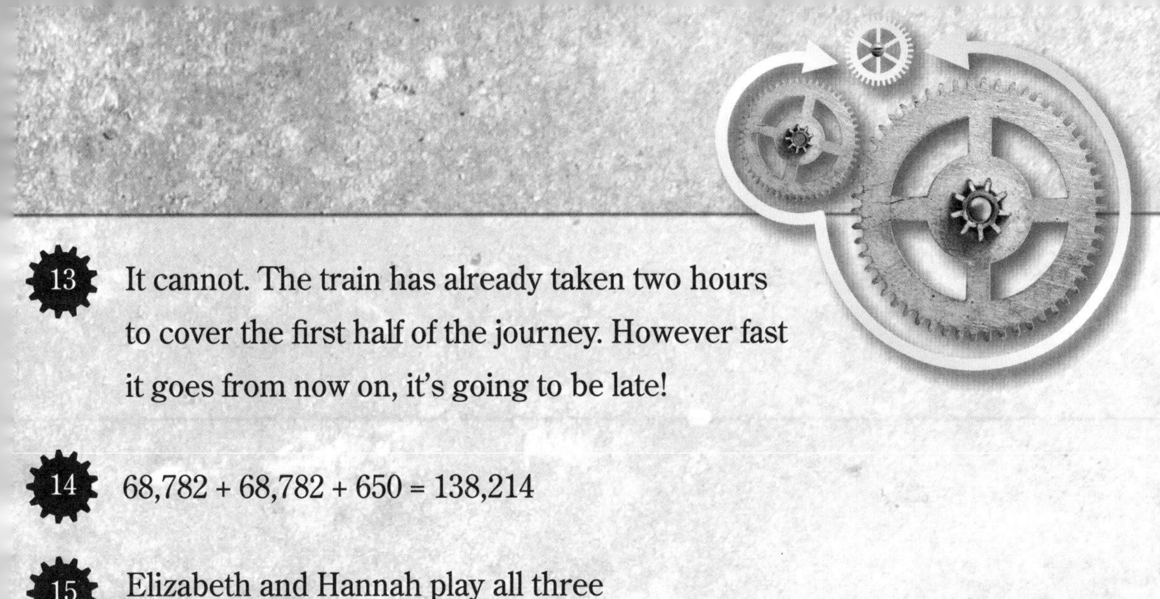

13 It cannot. The train has already taken two hours to cover the first half of the journey. However fast it goes from now on, it's going to be late!

14 68,782 + 68,782 + 650 = 138,214

15 Elizabeth and Hannah play all three instruments. James plays none of them.

16

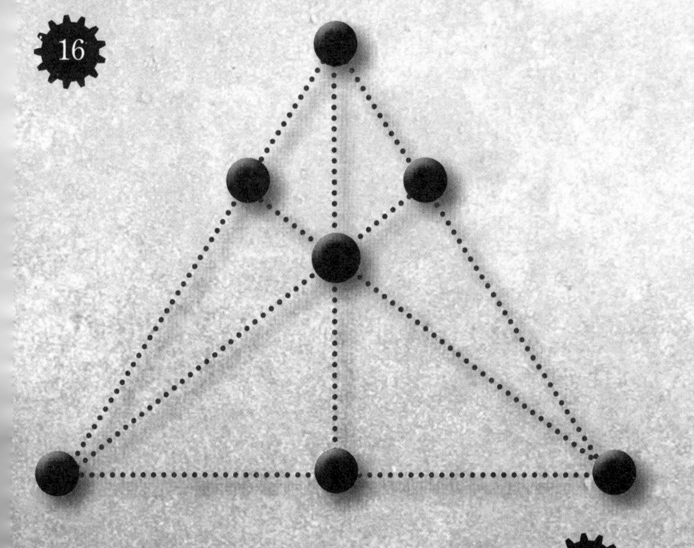

17 She makes a fruit salad!

18

19 There are three different colors, so he must take out at least four socks to be sure of a matching pair.

20 Zero. One of the terms is $(x - x)$, which is 0, and any number multiplied by zero is zero.

21 It takes eight days. It starts the eighth day at 7 feet up, and reaches the top at nightfall on that day.

22 There are 30 rectangles in total. (Remember that squares are a kind of rectangle.)

23 Just one. After that, the glass is no longer empty!

24

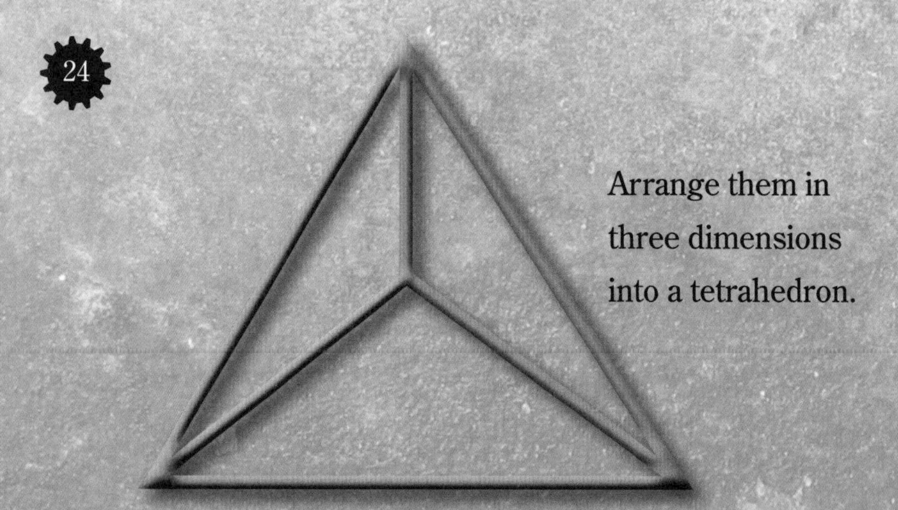

Arrange them in three dimensions into a tetrahedron.

25 There are 54 games. Each game results in one player leaving the tournament, so for n competitors, there will be $(n - 1)$ games.

26 She can score 100 using six arrows:
17 + 17 + 17 + 17 +16 + 16 = 100

The contestant should switch. She stands a ⅓ chance of winning if she sticks to her original choice, but a ⅔ chance if she switches. To see how this must be, think of it this way: When she made her original choice, there was a ⅓ chance that the car was behind door 1. Being told that behind one of the other doors is a goat does not change these odds—she already knew that. At the time of making the original choice, the odds that the car is behind either door 2 or door 3 are ⅔. After being shown the goat, she now knows that it is not door 3, so now the odds that it is door 2 are ⅔.

The same: $1,224.45 per year.

27 + 56 = 83
40 + 16 = 56
93 + 16 = 109

13112221

Reading what you see, the series is 'One 1', 'Two 1', One 2, Two 1', etc.

For each round of picking up sticks, Alexander must make sure that the number adds up to four. So if Graham picks up one stick, Alexander picks up three. If Graham picks up two sticks, Alexander also picks up two. If Graham picks up three, Alexander picks up one. By doing this, Alexander is ensuring that after five rounds, 20 sticks will have been picked up, leaving 1 stick left, which Graham must pick up.

If he tosses the coin twice, he knows that, whatever the bias, HT (heads then tails) is as likely as TH. So he tosses it twice. If it comes up HT, he goes to the bar. If it comes up TH, he stays at home. If it comes up HH or TT, he tosses the coin twice more. And so on until he gets either HT or TH.

36 Spike runs 8 miles in the hour.
He's running at 8 miles per hour, after all!

37 10. The pattern here is alternately adding
3 and then subtracting 2.

38 They are both the same length!

39 There are seven sea lions on the larger rock and five on the smaller rock. You can figure this out by making the following equations, where a is the larger group and b is the smaller group:

$a + 1 = 2(b - 1)$

$a - 1 = b + 1$

40 It would take him 24 days. In 8 days, Carter can mow ⅔ of the lawns, so Lewis mows ⅓ of the lawns in 8 days. This means that Lewis could mow all the lawns in 3 x 8 days.

41

42

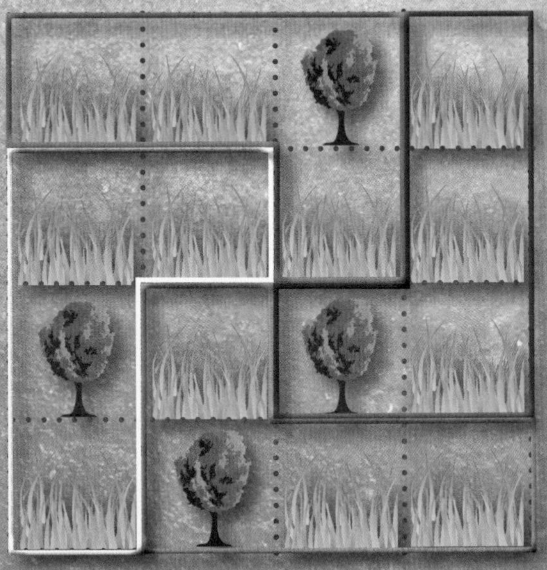

43

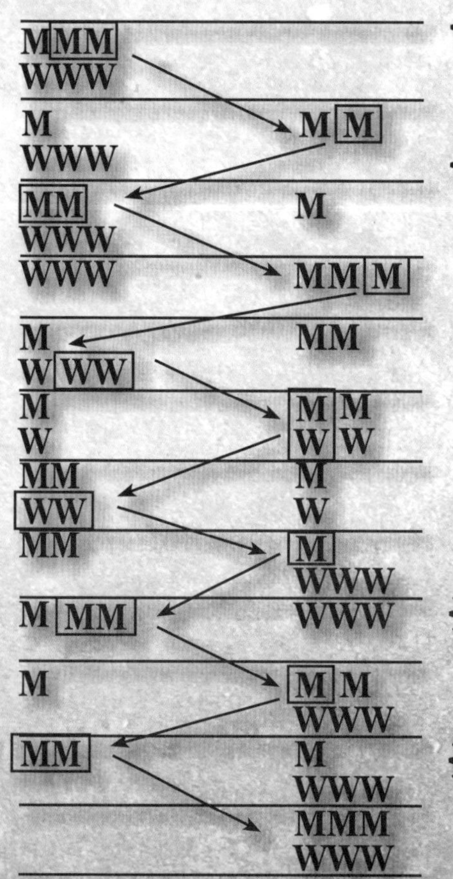

44 The grandmother she is talking about is her father's mother.

45 They are exactly the same shade of gray! We are fooled into thinking that there is a shadow on a regular board of white and gray squares, so we compensate accordingly. To see that this is really true, try covering up the other squares.

46 Once, since it is the same size as the first gear.

47 Counterclockwise. The first, third, and fifth gears will turn clockwise, and the second and fourth gears will turn anticlockwise.

48 The sister on the left cannot be Anne, since that would make Anne a liar. The sister in the middle cannot be Anne either, for the same reason. So the sister on the right must be Anne. Anne tells the truth, so the sister in the middle is Beatrix. That makes the sister on the left Caroline.

49

50 He crosses his arms before taking hold of the rope. When he uncrosses his arms, he will make a knot in the rope.

51 41 in. Since the books stand in the shelf, page 1 of Volume 1 and the last page of Volume 10 are not at the end of the stack!

52 When he takes the marble out of the bag, Gordon should cover it with his hand, put it straight into his mouth, and swallow it. The Inner Circle will then look at the other marble, see that it is black, and conclude that Gordon has swallowed the white marble. Lord Sleight will have to accept the decision or he would be exposed as a cheat!

53 $11^3 = 1{,}331$

54 Mrs. Thomas's backyard is three times the size of Mrs. Brown's backyard.

55 Did you spot the mistake? If not, turn back and read it again.

56 He is buying the brass numbers for his front door.

57

58 Let the distance AC, the radius of the larger circle, be x. CD = x - 9 and EC = x - 5. x - 5 is the mean proportional between the points x - 9 and x, a property derived from similar triangles. This means that $(x - 9)/(x - 5) = (x - 5)/x$, therefore $x = 25$. So the larger circle has a diameter of 50 in., and the smaller circle has a diameter of 41 in.

59 The four drinkers are a man and his sister plus his daughter and her son (or her daughter and his son).

60 The 14-inch pizza is a better deal. You're getting 49π square inches of pizza for \$10, or 4.9π per dollar. With the special offer, you get 50π for \$10.50, or 4.76π per dollar.

61

62 He starts both timers running at the same time. When the 4-minute timer runs out, he turns it over right away. When the 7-minute one runs out, he turns that over right away, too. Then when the 4-minute timer runs out for the second time, meaning 8 minutes are up, he turns the 7-minute timer over. This timer has only been running for one minute, so when it runs out again, 9 minutes are up.

63

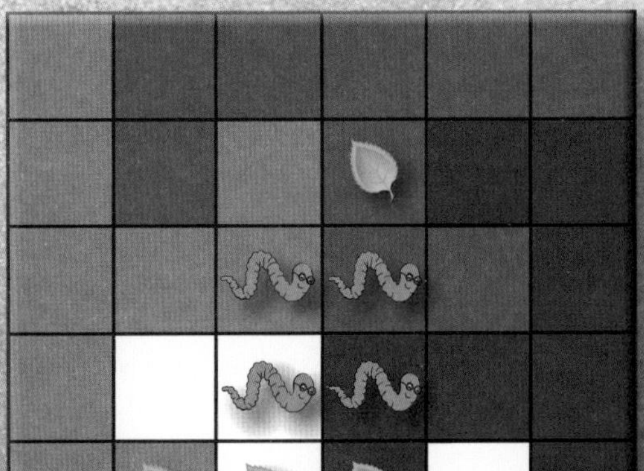

64 He is 50 inches tall.

65 First the farmer pours the lentils into the brewer's sack. He then binds the sack tightly and turns it inside out. Next, he pours the grain into the sack. Finally, he unbinds the sack and pours the lentils back into his own sack.

66 $\frac{7}{12}$. $58\frac{1}{3}$ percent is $58\frac{1}{3}/100$. Multiply both sides by 3 and you get 175/300, which is 7/12.

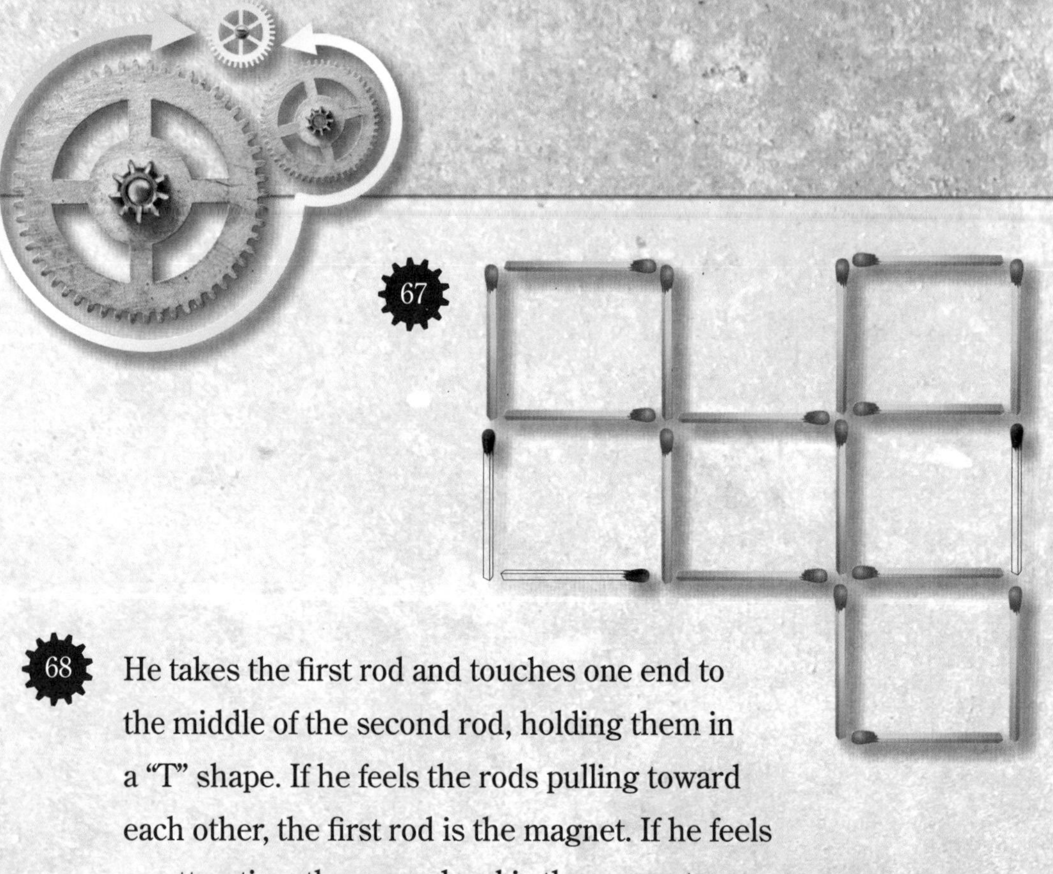

68 He takes the first rod and touches one end to the middle of the second rod, holding them in a "T" shape. If he feels the rods pulling toward each other, the first rod is the magnet. If he feels no attraction, the second rod is the magnet. This works because the center of a magnet does not pull iron objects toward it, but both ends of a magnet—its north and south poles—do.

69 5,050. The sum can be expressed in 50 pairs, all of which add up to 101: (100 + 1), (99 + 2) … (51 + 50). So the sum is the product of 50 x 101 = 5,050

70 It is 5 paces across. The two distances he has walked form the shorter sides of a right-angled triangle. The diameter is the hypotenuse of the triangle. As we know from Pythagoras, its square is equal to the squares of the other two sides: $3^2 + 4^2 = 5^2$

71

72 None. It's a hole!

73 The minimum number of turns needed is four. Here are the four turns you need to make: RBG, RGY, RBY, BGY. You've now turned each card three times, so they are all upside down. This will work whichever order you carry out the four turns in.

74 7. Each entry is the square of the previous entry.

75 The key fact to remember is that he can safely leave the wolf alone with the grain. First, he crosses the river with the goat. He leaves the goat on its own and comes back. Next trip, he takes the wolf across, but comes back with the goat. Now he takes the grain across, leaving the goat on its own again. Leaving the wolf with the grain on the far side of the river, he finally returns to pick up the goat.

76 

77 20 times.

78 Yes, once. To see this, imagine two climbers each setting off at the same time on the same day. They will have to pass each other somewhere along the route, no matter what speed they are going at.

They are parallel!

The house is at the South Pole.

The wallaby will win. It completes the race in 100 hops. The kangaroo needs 68 hops to complete the race since its 34th hop will take it 2 feet past the pole. At the moment the wallaby reaches the finishing line, the kangaroo will be in midair as it takes its 67th hop.

He needs to cut the wood into three pieces. Labeling the corners as below, first he measures the midpoint between B and C, which we will call A. He then draws lines from A to E and A to D and cuts along those lines, placing the pieces back together as shown.

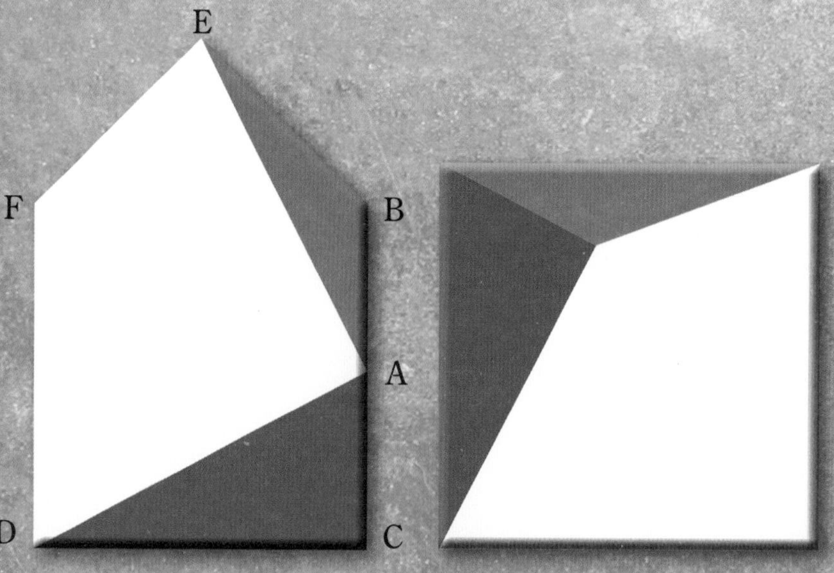

There are 31 squares.

The original order was 3, 5, 4, 2, as seen from Geraldine's perspective.

85

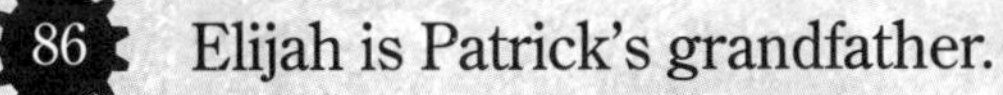

86 Elijah is Patrick's grandfather.

87 There are several possible combinations, but they all take at least four turns. For instance, you could change row 2, then column A, then column D, then row 4.

88

The trick is to view this as a 3-D image in perspective. Then the scales balance!

89 First fold the paper into a concertina shape. The paper will then take the book's weight without crumpling.

90

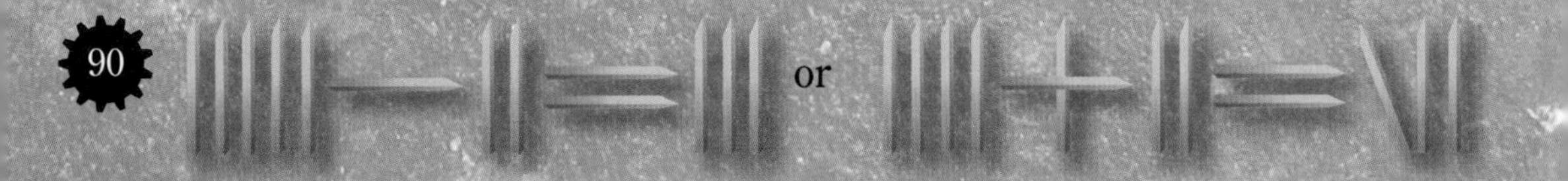

91 None! As Mr. Herman knows all too well, his mill has closed down.

92

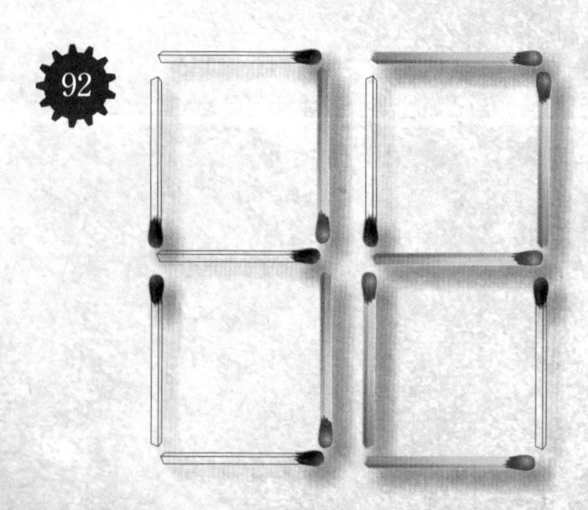

93 It weighs 1 pound.

94 545+5=550

95 It was the middle of the day.
Nobody said anything about nighttime!

96 They are onto a sure-fire winner! They may not be able to see their own hats, but they can see each other's. One guesses that his hat is the same color as the other's: if he sees black, he guesses black. The other guesses that his hat is a different color: if he sees black, he guesses red. Their hats must be either the same color or different colors, so one of them—and only one—is guaranteed to be right.

97

98 They are both the same distance from Abigail's house when they meet!

99 2,999. Divide 29 by 9, and that's how many 9s there are in the number. The remainder, 2, comes first.

100 There are two: a duck and a rabbit. But keep staring at it. Can you see both the duck and the rabbit at the same time, or do you only ever see one or the other?

101 There were 11 people at the party. The first person toasts with 10 others, the second 9, etc., so the total number of clinks is 10 + 9 + 8 + 7 + 6 + 5 + 4 + 3 + 2 + 1 = 55

102 He is lying. Bill's statement cannot be true because if it were, he would have told a truth, which contradicts the statement. It must be the case that he sometimes—but not always—lies, and that he is lying on this occasion.

103 The rectangle has an area of 2 units. The square needs an area of 2 units, too. This means that the square has sides that are $\sqrt{2}$ long. Slicing the rectangle into four triangles with a hypotenuse of $\sqrt{2}$ does the trick.

104 This time the area of the rectangle is 5 units, so the square needs sides that are $\sqrt{5}$. Four triangles with sides of 1, 2, and $\sqrt{5}$ can be made, plus a small square for them to fit around.

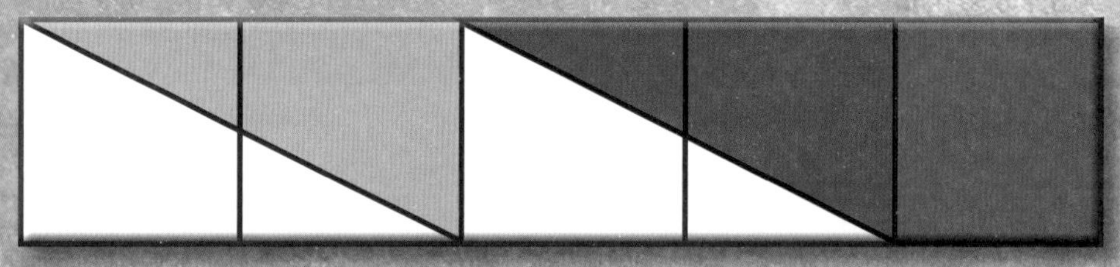

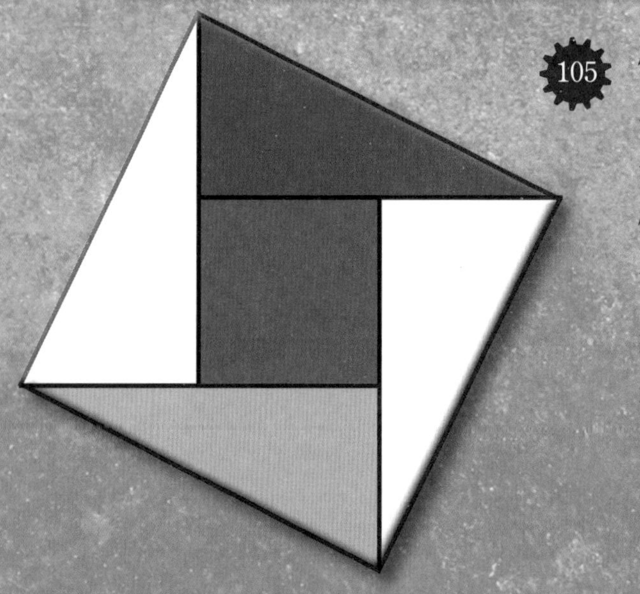

105 There are 36 pairs of times when the hands exactly change places between 3 p.m. and midnight. The number of pairs of times between hour n and midnight is equal to the sum of all the numbers from 1 to $(12 - (n + 1))$. Here, $n = 3$, so the answer is the sum of all the numbers up to 8: $1 + 2 + 3 + 4 + 5 + 6 + 7 + 8 = 36$

In this case, half of 13 is 8. Write out the numbers in Roman numerals, then chop them in half!

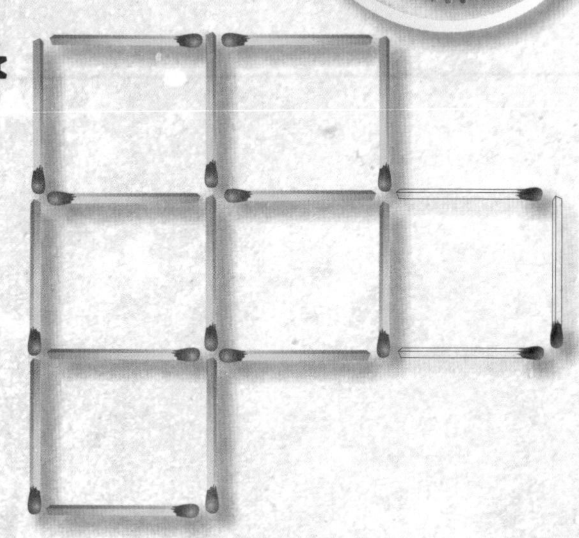

He will need 8 bags, containing the following amounts:

1, 2, 4, 8, 16, 32, 64, 12

To solve this, you need the series $2^0 + 2^1 + 2^2 ... + 2^6$, which gives a total of 127. With those you can make any number up to 127. Add the bag of 12, and you can make any number up to 139.

$1 + 2 + 3 + 4 + 5 + 6 + 7 + (8 \times 9) = 100$

She has 3 chickens and 6 pigs.

To solve this, make x the number of chickens, y the number of pigs.

$x + y = 9$; $2x + 4y = 30$ Solving the equations, $y = 6$, $x = 3$

The water level goes down. While the anchor is in the boat, it displaces an amount of water equal to its weight. When it is dropped overboard, the anchor only displaces an amount of water equal to its volume.

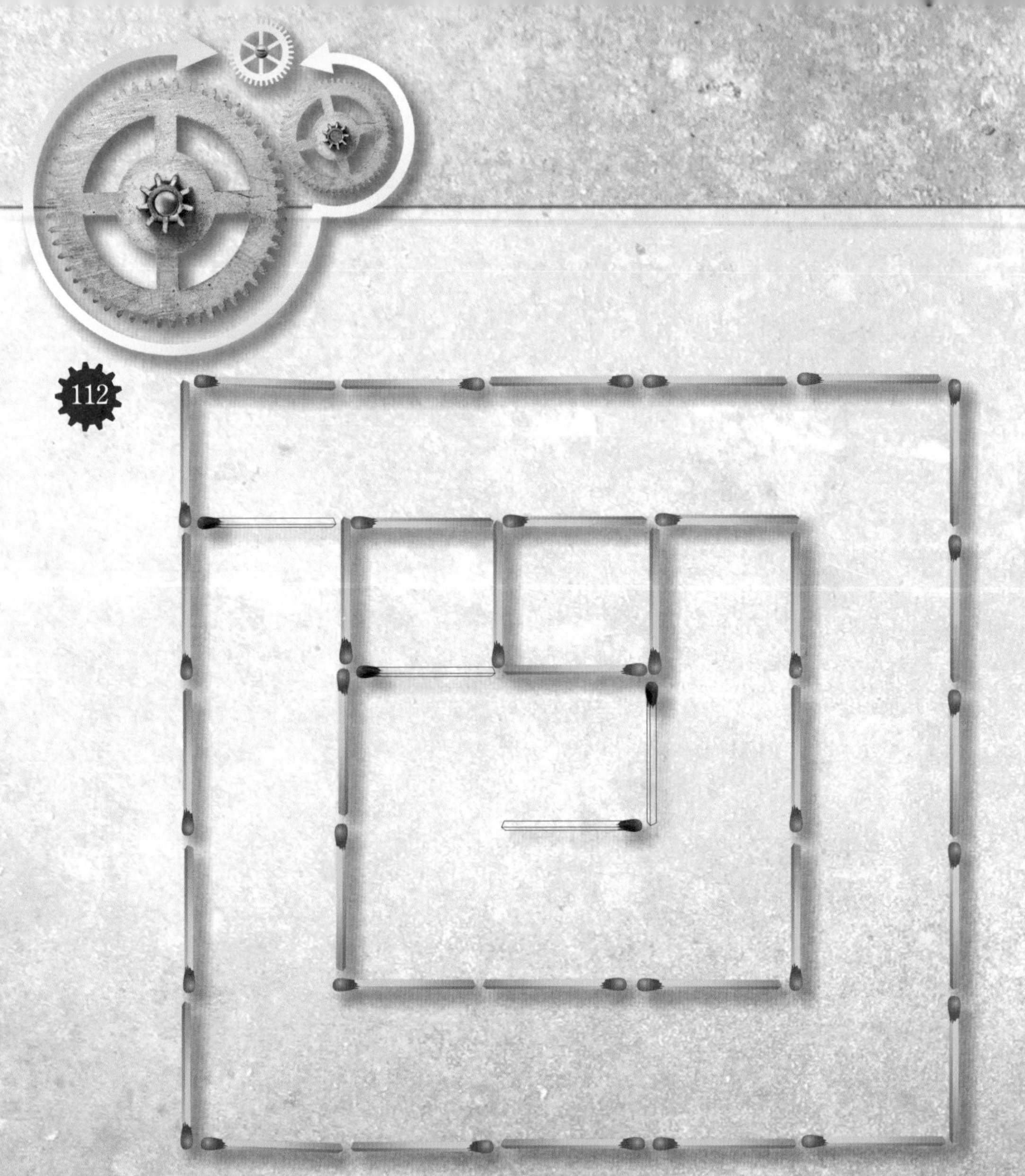

112

113 He should order two cogs from Mr. Black and six from Mr. Smith. He'll have his eight cogs in two weeks.

114 None. He finished fourth!

115 Not 35 minutes! If she can ride 12 miles in 30 minutes with the wind, she can ride 16 miles in 40 minutes with the wind. Against the wind, she manages 12 miles in 40 minutes. So her speed without any wind would be 14 miles in 40 minutes. She only needs to cycle 12 miles, so it takes her $12 \times {}^{40}\!/_{14}$ minutes, which is 34 minutes, 28 $^{2}\!/_{7}$ seconds.

She lights one wick at one end, and at the same time lights the other wick at both ends. When the second wick has burned all the way down, she knows that half an hour has passed. At that moment, she lights the other end of the second wick. When this second wick has burned down, she knows that 45 minutes will have passed.

They weren't playing each other!

If she sells everything, Mrs. Smith will get 24 cents. She will give Mrs. Bramley 15 cents for her apples, leaving Mrs. Smith with 9 cents. But Mrs Smith's 30 apples were worth 10 cents to her, so she's cheated herself out of a penny.

$5^7 = 78{,}125$

120

1 lb., 3 lb., 9 lb., and 27 lb.

He can put the weights on either side of the balance scale:

1 lb. = 1 lb.; 2 lb. = 3 lb. – 1 lb.; 3 lb. = 3 lb. ...

39 lb. = 27 lb. + 9 lb. + 3 lb.; 40 lb. = 27 lb. + 9 lb. + 3 lb. + 1 lb.

122

200 in. If you rolled out the cylinder into a flat rectangle, it would look like this. The line traces the path of four diagonal lines. Each line is the hypotenuse of a right-angled triangle with one side 40 in. and the other 30 in. (120 ÷ 4). Using Pythagoras' theorem, we see that the line is 4 x 50 in. = 200 in. long

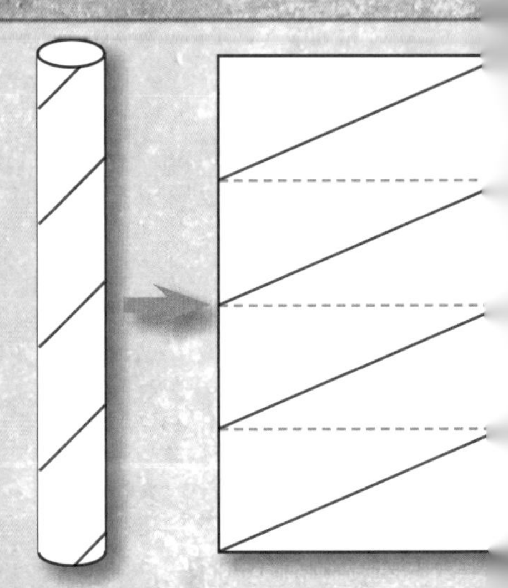

123

135 = (1 + 3 + 5) x 1 x 3 x 5

124

First she turns two switches to the "on" position and leaves them there for five minutes. Then she turns one of these two switches off and goes downstairs. She knows that the bulb that is on is controlled by the switch that is on. She feels the other two bulbs. The bulb that is warm is controlled by the switch she turned on and then off again. The bulb that is cold is controlled by the switch that she has not turned on at all.

125

They must both be lying. If only one had been lying, they would both have said that they were boys or both have said that they were girls. So you know that the child with blue eyes is the girl and the child with brown eyes is the boy.

126

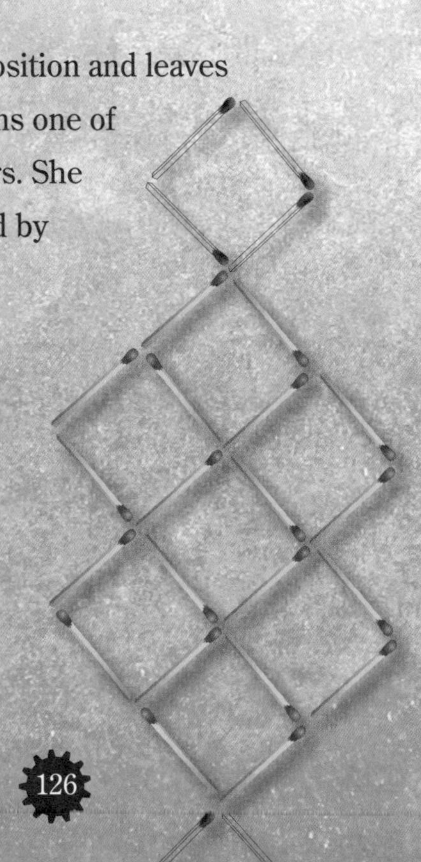

The prisoner said: "I will face the firing squad."
The king could not deem the statement true or false.
If he deems it true, it cannot come true. If he deems it false, it must come true. Bewildered, the king gives the prisoner a pardon.

888 + 88 + 8 + 8 + 8 = 1,000

They are a nine-year-old and two twins age of two. As their product is 36, they could only be the ages of nine, two, and two or six, six, and one. Upon finding out that there is an eldest, the census taker knows that they must be nine, two, and two.

A decimal point. It gives you 4.9.

We know that Mr. Blue must be wearing either a black or red shirt. But the man in the black shirt replied to the first man, calling him Mr. Blue. This means that Mr. Blue must be in the red shirt. The man in the black shirt can only be Mr. Blue or Mr. Red, but Mr. Blue is in the red shirt, so we know that the man in the black shirt must be Mr. Red. This leaves the man who didn't speak as Mr. Black wearing a blue shirt.

The carpenter uses 96 nails. Each corner needs one nail, then each side has 23 more.

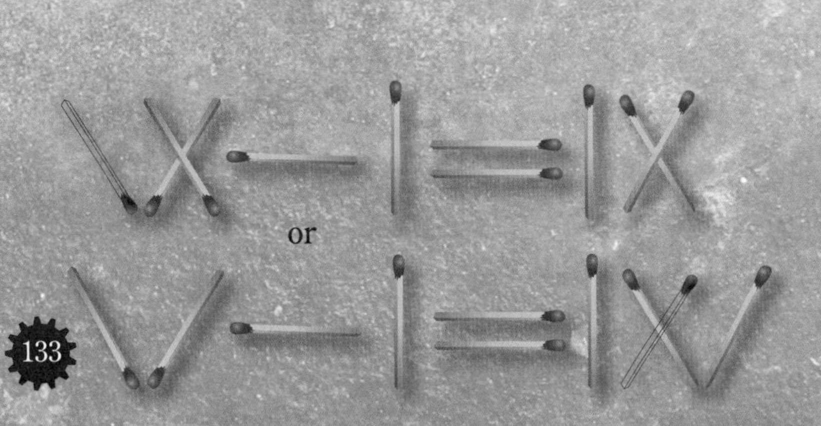

134 There are eight teams in the League. If they played each other only once, the first team would play seven other teams, the second would play six, etc. So the total would be 7 + 6 + 5 + 4 + 3 + 2 + 1 = 28 However, they play each other twice, so 28 x 2 = 56

135 He should ask: "Which door would the other guard tell me was the door to freedom?" He then chooses the other door.

136 The total is 4,100. Did you make it 5,000? Don't worry, most people do.

137 Edward!

138 First he fills flask A with blood from flask C. Then he pours the contents of flask A into flask B. Next, he fills flask A again with blood from flask C. He fills flask B from flask A and pours out what is left in flask A. Now he fills flask A from flask B. This leaves 2 pints in flask B and 2 pints in flask C. Pouring the contents of flask B into flask C gives him his 4 pints.

140 He takes a piece of wood and lights it on the fire. He then returns to a point a few yards in from the east end of the island and starts a fire there. This new fire will burn all the way across to the east coast, and the man can take shelter in the area it burns out. What he does for food after the fire has burned out is another question!

60 feet.

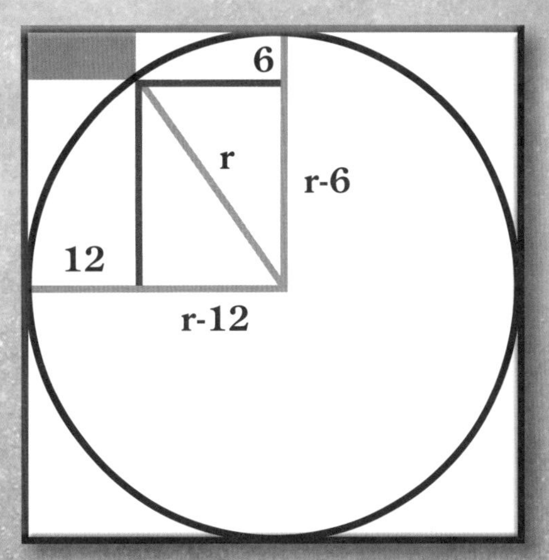

To find the radius, you need to make a right-angle triangle with the radius as the hypotenuse. So, using Pythagoras' theorem, $(r - 6)^2 + (r - 12)^2 = r^2$. This simplifies to: $r^2 - 36r + 180 = 0$. On factorizing, we get: $(r - 30)(r - 6) = 0$; so: $r = 30$ or 6. However, we can reject the solution $r = 6$ as this would give a negative length $(r - 12)$. So, $r = 30$, the diameter $= 2 \times 30 = 60$

142 She gives 23 of the children a candy, and gives the 24th child the bag with the last piece still in it.

34. Each term is the sum of the two previous terms. This is known as the Fibonacci series, and it crops up a lot in nature.

The figure of the girl at the front is the largest. The perspective lines fool us into thinking that the top figure is larger because we perceive it to be farther away.

Look carefully at the large figures. The red and blue triangles have different slopes, so neither of the large figures is a triangle. The bottom figure in fact bulges up slightly along the red–blue side, while the top figure sinks in slightly. This is how area A appears.

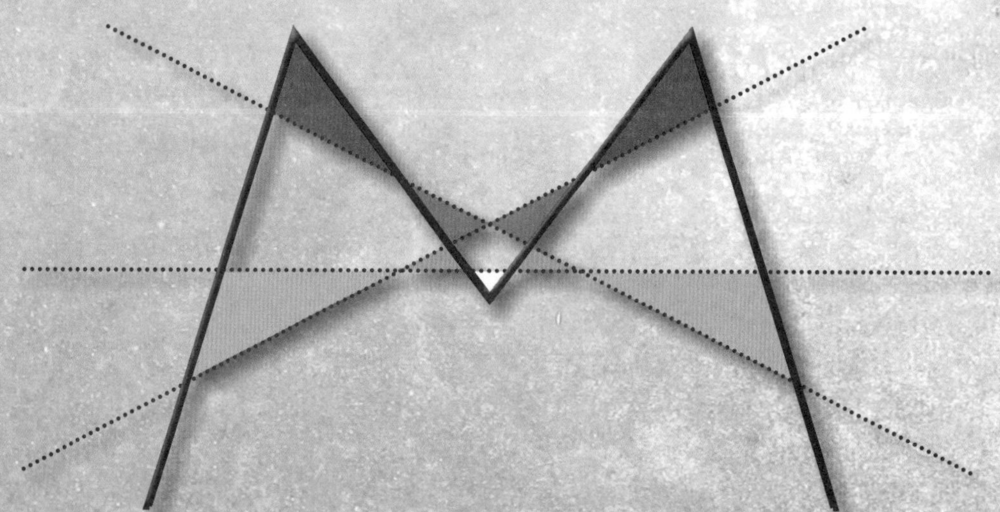

He must break the chocolate 31 times. There are 32 squares. He starts off with one piece, and each time he breaks a piece, he increases the number of pieces he has by one, so he must break the chocolate (32 - 1) times to get 32 separate pieces.

You need just 6.28 feet more rope. The radius of the circle has been increased by 1 foot. The circumference of a circle is $2\pi r$. So the extra rope you need is 2π feet, or approximately 6.28.

5 dollars.

9,567 + 1,085 = 10,652

They are both perfectly round!

In one hour, the pool gets $\frac{5}{60} + \frac{12}{60} + \frac{6}{60} + \frac{10}{60}$ full, which equals $\frac{33}{60}$. It will be completely full in $\frac{60}{33}$ hours = 1 hour, 49 minutes, and $6\frac{2}{3}$ seconds.

156 She bought 18 eggs. The farmer offered her 16 for 12 cents and threw in 2 extra. The original offer would have been 9 cents a dozen. The second offer was 8 cents a dozen.

157 9 marbles. Top scale shows:
shell (s) + 3 cubes (c) = 12 marbles (m), so $c = 4m - \frac{1}{3}s$
Substituting into the middle scale, we see that $4s/3 = 12m$

158 15 minutes. Relative to the carriage, he is driving at 8 mph. When he stops, it will be catching up with him at 8 mph, or 2 miles per 15 minutes, so he needs to drive long enough to get ahead by 2 miles, which is 15 minutes.

159 They are both married, but not to each other!

160 Opinions vary about this paradox, but here is one way to look at it. As Euthalus has not yet won a case, the court will necessarily have to rule against Protagoras, so Euthalus will not have to pay. However, if Protagoras were to bring another case, he would surely win that case, and Euthalus would have to pay. Alternatively, Euthalus could get another lawyer to represent him in court!

161

162 His father!

163 The most likely result is an approximation to π (pi), which is roughly 3.14!

164 Andrea is 20 years old. Her mother is 40.
Ten years ago, Andrea was 10 and her mother was 30.

165

166 He seats the clerks back-to-back.

167 There is no missing dollar. The travelers spent \$27 altogether, not \$30. Of that \$27, \$25 went to the hotel, and \$2 to the bellhop.

168 The cabin is the cabin of a plane.
The men died in a plane crash.

169 By the time the truck has driven the 5 miles to the center of the bridge, it has burned more than 1 pound in weight of fuel, so even with the pigeon on it, it is still under the 20-ton limit.

170 The chances that both the children were girls are ½, or 50:50. Calling the children child 1 and child 2, there are four possibilities (child 1 comes first): GG, GB, BG, and BB. After finding out that one is a girl, clearly, BB is impossible. If child 1 is the girl we know about, then only possibilities GB and GG are possible. If child 2 is the girl we know about, only possibilities BG and GG are possible. In both cases, there is a 50:50 chance of GG.

171

172 You don't bury survivors!

173 He picks up the second glass, pours its contents into the fifth glass, then places the second glass back where it was.

174 He should put one white marble in one bowl, and the rest of the marbles in the other. That way, he is guaranteed a pardon if he chooses the right bowl, and he has a 49/99 chance if he chooses the wrong one, giving him a nearly 3/4 chance of survival.

175 There are two possible solutions:
5,795 + 6,435 + 2,505 = 14,735 or 5,305 + 2,475 + 6,595 = 14,375

176 There were just three men: a man, his father, and his grandfather.

177

178 2 minutes. When the front of the train enters the tunnel, the back is 1 mile away, so the train needs to travel 2 miles until the back of the train reaches the end of the tunnel. The train is traveling at 1 mile per minute, so it takes 2 minutes to pass through the tunnel.

179 You need to turn over the 8 and the brown card. You are only testing whether or not even cards are red. The red card could be even or odd without disproving the statement. This test was devised by psychologist Peter Cathcart Wason. Most people get it wrong!

180 They tip the cask over so that the wine level reaches the brim. If they can see the bottom of the cask, Dee the pessimist has got it right. If not, Dum the optimist is correct.

181 First he numbers the bottles 1 to 12. He takes one pill from bottle 1, two from bottle 2, three from bottle 3, up to 12 from bottle 12. He now has 78 pills in total. If all the pills are aspirin, they will weigh 780 grams. If bottle 1 is arsenic, then one of the pills will be arsenic, and they will weigh 779 g. If bottle 2 is arsenic, they will weigh 778 g, etc. So by subtracting the reading on the scale from 780, he will arrive at the number of the bottle containing the arsenic.

182 The ladder has 23 rungs.

183 13 x 4 = 52

184

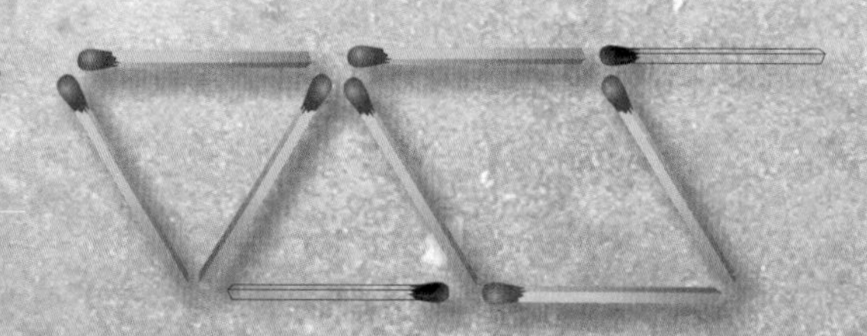

185 2 hours 15 minutes.

186 Two. Only Mrs. Tyler was going to the market!

187 The case is a rectangle 4 ft. long and 3 ft. wide. It has an outside diagonal 5 ft. long, and an inside diagonal a little bit shorter than that (allowing for the width of the wood). So it can carry a cue that is nearly 5 ft. long.

188 40

189 Still 40. There are 13 different kinds of card in each suit, so the slowest way to draw 4 of a kind is (13 x 3) + 1. This is true however many decks of cards you are drawing from.

190 They are both the same size!

191 There are two possible solutions:
5,832/17,496 or 5,823/17,469

She breaks all the links in one of the short chains and uses them to link the other three together. That way, she has to break only three links.

193 60 degrees. Imagine a third line as shown on the right. The three lines now make an equilateral triangle, which has three internal angles of 60 degrees.

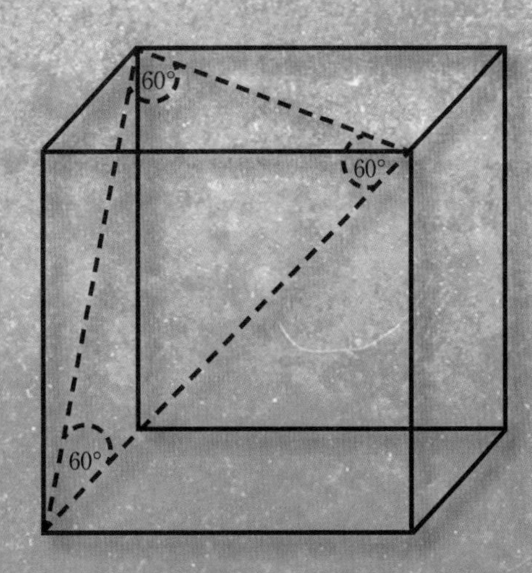

194 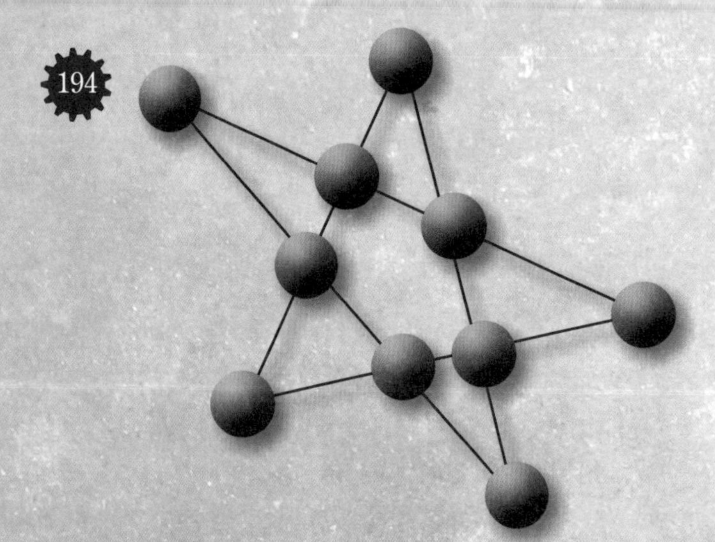

195 He puts one of the diamonds in the small box, then puts the small box and the other two diamonds in the big box. Alternatively, he puts all three diamonds in the small box then puts it in the big box.

196 (5 x 5 x 5) - (5 x 5) = 100

197 Roger is 40. Matthew is four and Theresa is one.

198 It is 9 p.m.

199 By turning the book upside down!
X = I + IX

200 You need to make six slices. Each slice reveals one face of the small cube at the center of the larger cube. Once all six of its faces have been revealed, all 27 cubes will have been separated.

201 Since all the labels are wrong, the box labeled "gold or silver" must be the box containing the bronze coins. Therefore, the box labeled "silver" must contain the gold, and the box labeled "gold" must contain the silver.

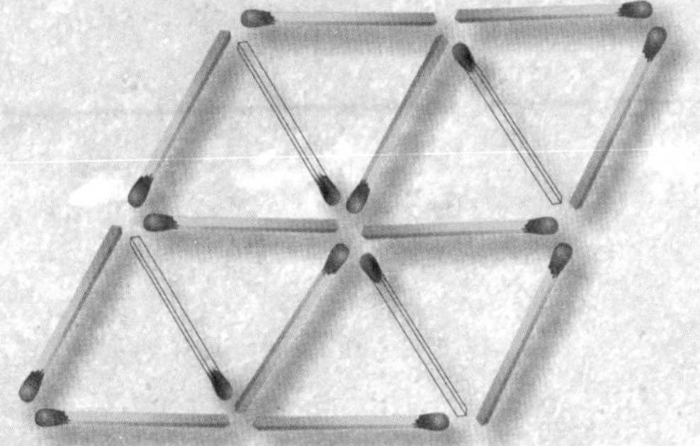

25 cents and 50 cents.
Only one of the coins is not a quarter, remember.

Do you see the circles rotate?

The carpet should be cut like this:

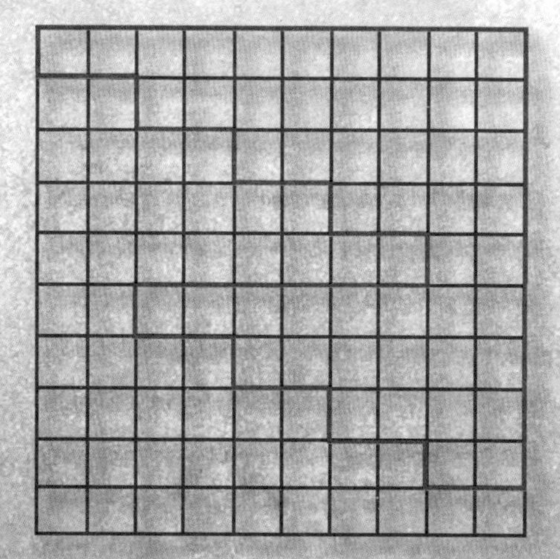

It will fit the room like this:

80. 30 divided by ½ equals 60.

They average exactly one pen each, so they have 360 pens between them.

Three.
She has lost two—her sight and her hearing.

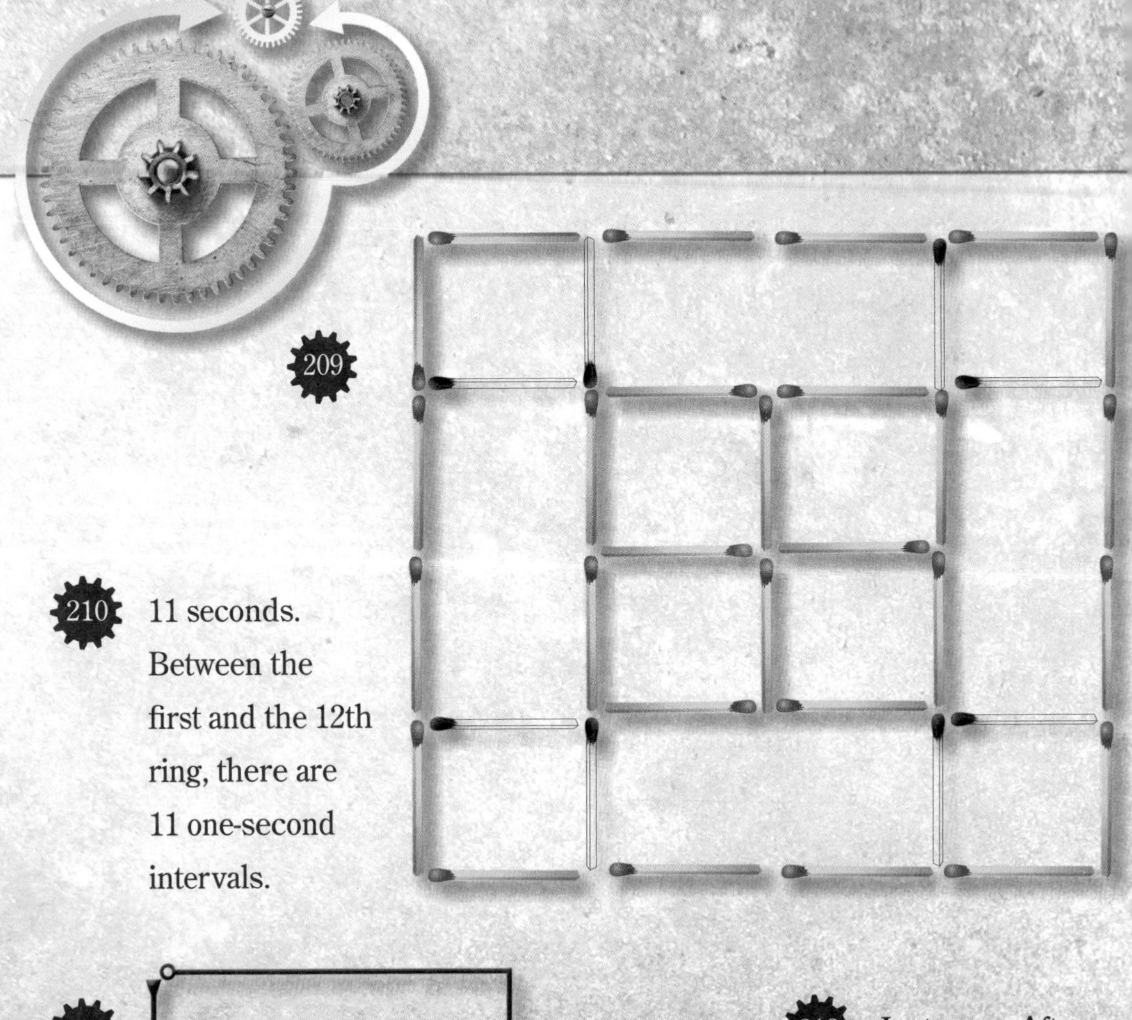

209

210 11 seconds. Between the first and the 12th ring, there are 11 one-second intervals.

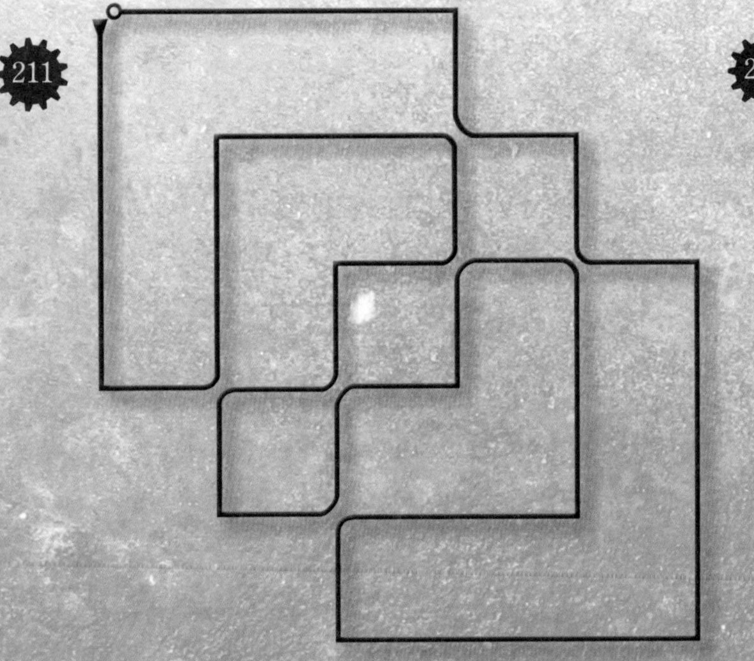

211

212 Just once. After that, you have 30, not 36.

If you are right-handed, you probably think the bottom figure is the happier. If you are left-handed, the top figure is likely to appear more cheerful. This test was devised by psychologist Julian Jaynes to show how our perception is affected by the left–right lateralization of our brains.

50 eggs. In eight days, 200 hens would lay on average 200 eggs, so in two days, they will lay a quarter of that number.

His horse is named Friday!

William has earned \$3.25 in all. He made \$2.25 in the first week, 75¢ in the second week, and only 25¢ in the third week.

At first, it probably looks as though the stairs lead up from right to left. But keep looking, and you will see an upside-down staircase, too. You cannot see both at the same time, however, and you should feel a distinct shift every time your brain switches from one interpretation of the image to the other. Do you see it switch when you blink?

$(1 + 9 + 6 + 8 + 3) \times (1 + 9 + 6 + 8 + 3) \times (1 + 9 + 6 + 8 + 3) = 19{,}683$

220 First he made a fold in the paper as shown by the dotted line. Taking points A and B, he drew semicircles alternately using B, then A, then B, then A as the center, being careful to make the ends join each time.

221 Cycling may be his profession, but on this particular day, he was driving his car!

222

223 It will take him at least six minutes. If you call the cakes A, B, and C, he bakes A and B on side 1, then A on side 2 and C on side 1, then finally B and C on side 2.

224

225 First he splits the stones into three groups of 27. He weighs two of the groups against each other. If one group is heavier than the other, he knows that the fake is in that group. If the two groups are balanced, he knows that the fake is in the group he did not weigh. Now he takes the group of 27 that contains the fake, splits it into three groups of nine, and repeats the process for the second weighing. He takes the resultant group of nine, and splits it into three groups of three for the third weighing. After three weighings, he has three stones left for his final weighing. He weighs two of them against each other. If one is heavier, that is the fake. If they are balanced, the stone he has not weighed is the fake.

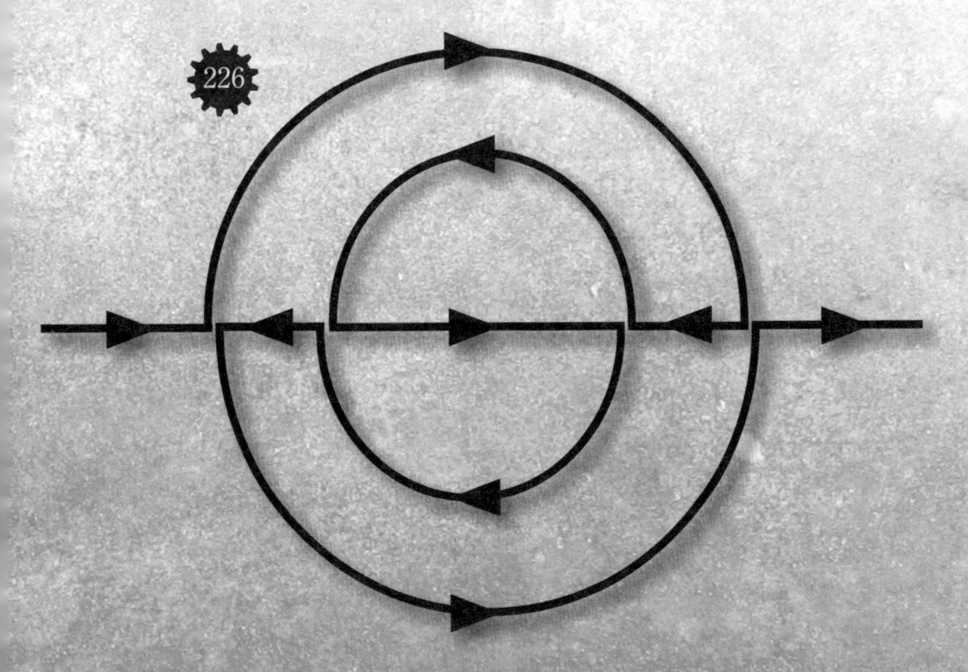

227 $3 \times 5,694 = 17,082$

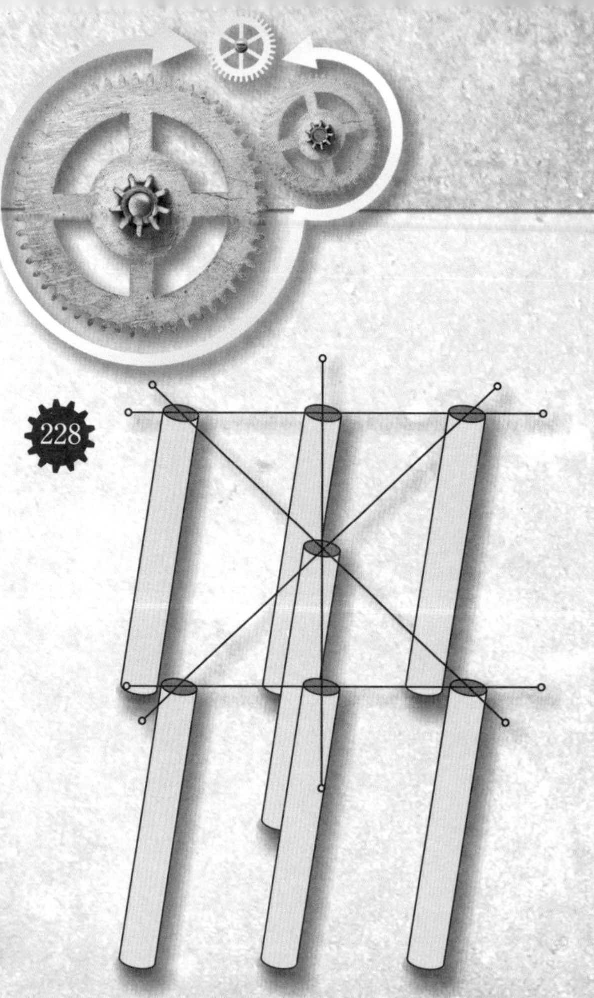

228

229 3,800

230 She says: "You will not give me the copper or silver coin." If this is true, you get the gold coin. It cannot be a lie, because if it were a lie, it would have to come true!

231 Here's one way to do it: They order ABCDD on night 1, finding out what D is; AEFGG on night 2, finding out G and A, which they had also ordered on night 1; and BEHII on night 3, finding out what I, B, and E are. This leaves C, F, and H, which they ordered once each. C is the unknown dish from night 1, F from night 2, and H from night 3.

232 He replies, "No, a sane person would pull out the plug!"

233

They have five children.

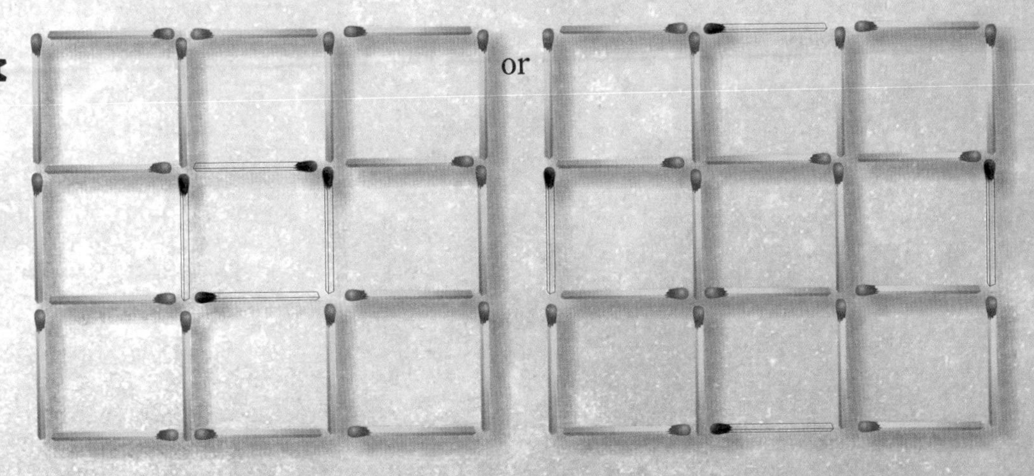

102 becomes 10^2, or 100, so
$101 - 10^2 = 1$

He divides the cards into piles of 42 and 10, then turns the whole pile of 10 over.

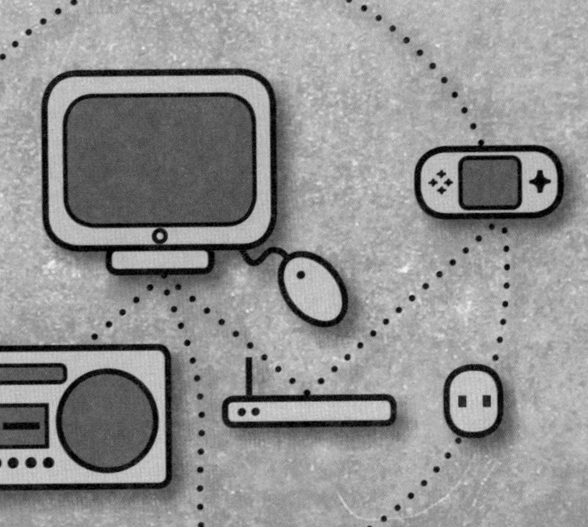

21 dollars.

Yes. He makes 10 dollars on each deal, so he is 20 dollars up at the end of the day.

He should choose to be thrown into the pit of lions. If the lions have not eaten for five months, they will be dead!

There will be 21 holes.

4 is a square number because it is 2 squared!

Emma won two games, and Jane won three games more than Emma, so they played a total of seven games.

They should open the gold box. If the will were in the silver box, all the inscriptions would be false. If it were in the lead box, all the inscriptions would be true.

177 – 77 = 100

He left the house at 7:05. The time he saw was 2 hr. 10 min. earlier than the real time. The mirror image is reflected across a symmetrical point of 6:00 (since this was morning). That means that the time he saw was 6:00 plus half of 2 hr. 10 min., which is 7:05. He thought the time was 4:55.

What we know:

	Before	Now
Mother	x	40
Son	y	z

$40 = 4y$, so $y = 10$

$z = x$

The difference in their ages is the same at all times, so:

$40 - x = x - 10$

This means that $x = 25$, so the son is 25 years old.

An hourglass.

After one team loses all its members, the team that it eliminates members from will always win. For example, if the red team is the first team to lose all its members, it is now impossible for the blue team to lose any members, so the blue team will eventually win. The best strategy is in fact to avoid answering questions until one team is eliminated, because any correct answer from one team will reduce the size of the second team that eliminates members from the third team. If all the players know this, none of them will ever answer correctly.

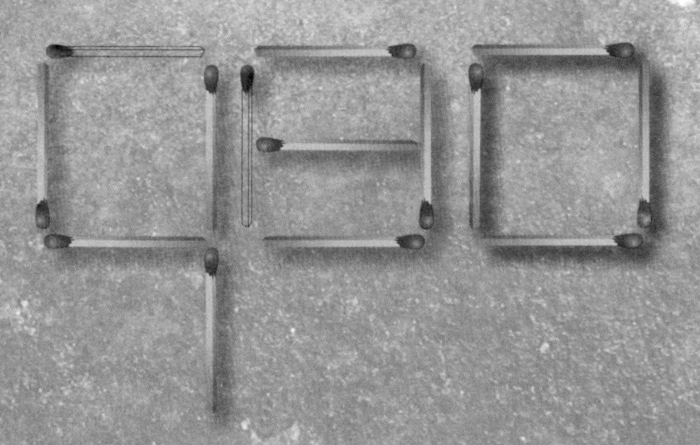

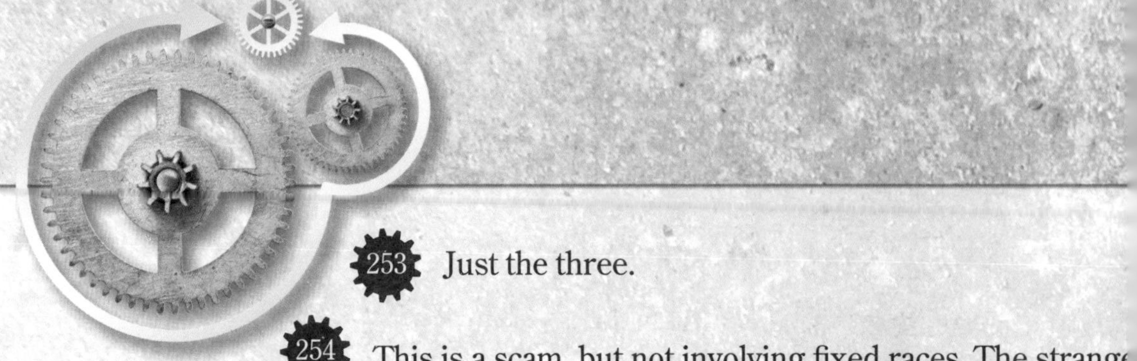

253 Just the three.

254 This is a scam, but not involving fixed races. The stranger has been sending out thousands of e-mails every day, giving different predictions involving all the runners in the race, then sending out another prediction just to those who received the correct result in the previous race. At the start of the week, he sent perhaps 10,000 e-mails. Now he is left with a dozen or so potential suckers, and you're one of them!

255 The baby weighs 25 lb.
The cat weighs 10 lb. and the woman weighs 135 lb.

256 2,178 x 4 = 8,712

257 She has two nephews and four nieces.
Beatrice has two daughters.
Carla has one son and two daughters.
Davina has one son.

258

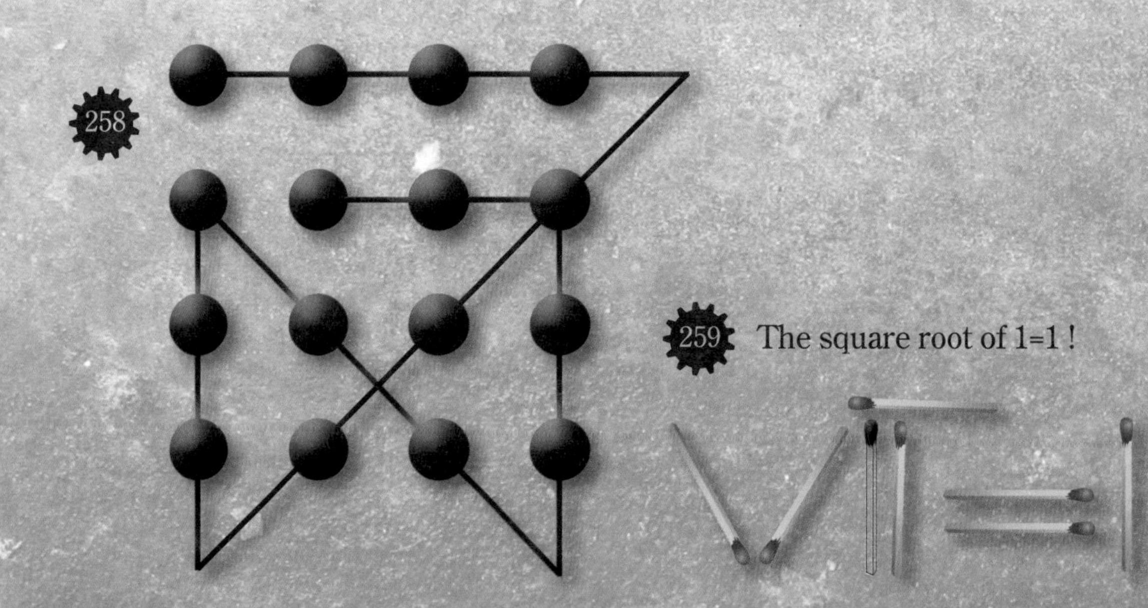

259 The square root of 1=1 !

 The boy should carry 40/100 of the whole weight, so the pig should be hung 60/100 the length of the pole from the boy's shoulder. This means that it should be hung 3 feet from the boy's shoulder and 2 feet from the father's shoulder.

 The spirit must be behind door D, meaning that just the inscription on door B is true.
If it were behind Door A, then B and D would be true.
If it were behind Door B, then A and D would be true.
If it were behind Door C, then A, C, and D would all true.

 $5 \times (5 - (1 \div 5)) = 24$

$1 \div 5 = 0.2$

$5 - 0.2 = 4.8$

$4.8 \times 5 = 24$

 The doctor is the boy's mother!

	6	4	
2	8	1	7
	5	3	

267

 The bear must be standing at the North Pole, so presumably it is a polar bear and it is white.

 6,438. The digits shift along one place each time, moving to the front when they reach the end.

The late-night movie finished in the middle of the night. In 72 hours' time, it will also be the middle of the night, so it won't be bright or sunny.

The room Sylvester has walked into is an elevator.

The calendar repeats itself every 28 years. The couple claim to have been married on that date 28 years ago, but the woman said they were married on a Sunday, and that date 28 years ago had to have been a Thursday.

81. Each term is the sum of the three preceding terms.

The three women share eight dishes, so they each consume $\frac{8}{3}$ dishes. Claire has only given away $\frac{1}{3}$ of a dish, while June has given away $2\frac{1}{3}$, which is seven times as much. So to be fair, Jennifer should pay June $7 and Claire just $1.

They were riding each other's horse.

It does not fall at all. His hands will meet in the middle of the pole!

-10. Each number is the previous number multiplied by -13.

Mother	Child	Age
Juliet	Jamie	3
Monica	Graham	4
Laura	Dylan	2
Anne	Holly	1

Here is one way to do it.

The rest of the officers lost their head—Captain Blighty!

You need four colors. In fact, you only need four colors for any map, real or imagined.

Bruce has a moustache and stole the watch. Watson has a beard and stole the purse. Crusoe is clean-shaven and stole the wallet.

285 He folds each corner of the paper into the center. This will give him a square that is exactly half the size of the original square, but double the thickness. He can do his painting on the opposite side of the paper to the folds.

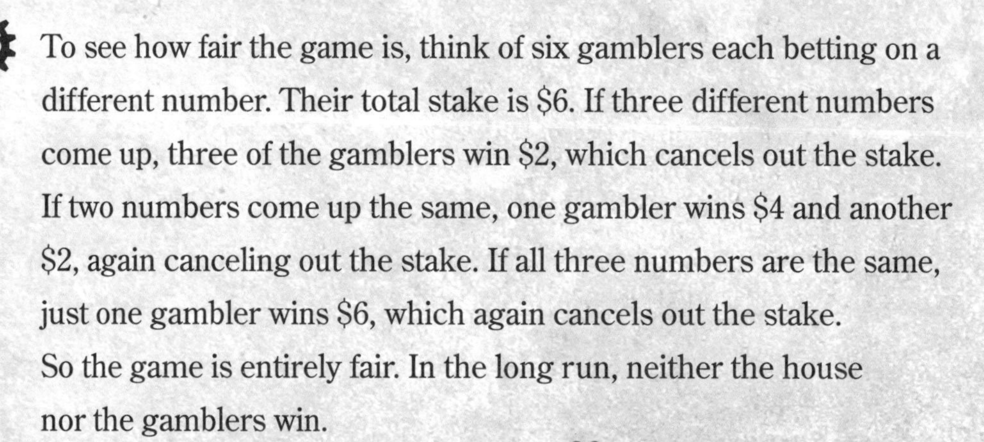

286 To see how fair the game is, think of six gamblers each betting on a different number. Their total stake is $6. If three different numbers come up, three of the gamblers win $2, which cancels out the stake. If two numbers come up the same, one gambler wins $4 and another $2, again canceling out the stake. If all three numbers are the same, just one gambler wins $6, which again cancels out the stake. So the game is entirely fair. In the long run, neither the house nor the gamblers win.

287

288

289 $1,089 \times 9 = 9,801$

290 None of the dots is actually there. If you focus on one intersection, the dot there disappears, but you can still see all the others.

291 He needs to be at least 1 foot away from the mirror. When you look at a mirror image, you see yourself as if the mirror image were the same distance behind the mirror as you are in front of it. So although James is only 1 foot from the mirror, the image of his face will look like it is 2 feet away, and it will be in focus.

292 There are now eight small diamonds and one large one.

293 The missing number is 6. The middle number of each set of three is the sum of the digits in the numbers on either side of it.

294 It has moved 8 feet. Before the slide, the top of the ladder was 24 feet up the wall. This is solved using Pythagoras' theorem: $24^2 = 25^2 - 7^2$. After the slide, the ladder is 20 feet up the wall. Therefore, the square of the distance from the wall to the base of the ladder is now $25^2 - 20^2 = 15^2$. So the distance moved is $15 - 7 = 8$ feet.

It is 12 o'clock noon. It is also time to buy a new clock!

By the time Grace joins in, Helen has peeled 10 potatoes, so there are 45 left. Six minutes later, Grace has peeled 30 and Helen 12, leaving 3 left. Grace takes another 24 seconds to peel two more and six seconds later Helen finishes the last one. In total, from the time Helen started peeling, it took them 11 minutes 30 seconds to finish them. Helen peeled 23 potatoes, while Grace peeled 32.

The next year will be 2307. Increasing the second and third digits by 1 gives you the next six years after that: 2417, 2527, 2637, 2747, 2857, 2967

The cork is floating to the highest point in the water, which is at the edge of the glass, where the water clings to the sides. But if you fill the glass completely, the water will bulge in a convex shape above the sides, and the cork will settle at the center.

The German owns the fish. Here is the full breakdown:

	Color	Nationality	Beverage	Smoke	Pet
1	Yellow	Norwegian	Water	Dunhill	Cats
2	Blue	Danish	Tea	Blends	Horse
3	Red	British	Milk	Pall Mall	Birds
4	Green	German	Coffee	Prince	Fish
5	White	Swedish	Beer	Bluemast	Dogs